This Sporting Day

RON BROWN

Down Memory Lane I linger long,
Till evening shadows fall,
To dream of golden days bygone,
And radiant hours recall.

MILESTONE PUBLICATIONS

Phototypesetting by Inforum Ltd., Portsmouth
Printed by R. J. Acford, Chichester

Published by Milestone Publications
The Publishing and Bookselling Division
of Goss & Crested China Limited
62 Murray Road Horndean Hants PO8 9JL

1st impression 1984

British Library Cataloguing in Publication Data

Brown, Ron
  This sporting life.—(Down memory lane; 9)
  1. Sports—England—Gosport (Hampshire)
  —History
  I. Title   II. Series
  796′09422′78   GV605.7.G6

ISBN 0-903852-23-3

ON YOUR MARKS

We are now living in a world in which the pursuit of leisure appears to be playing an increasingly important role, a state of affairs that may be attributed to more people having more time available in which to indulge their off-duty interests, and it would seem that because of the great advances in technology that are taking place, enter the microchip, we shall all be afforded far more time in the future.

Sport has always featured prominently in leisure and pleasure activities, and history shows that sporting facilities and achievements generally improve when the unemployment figures are at their highest, hence the steady rate that sports halls and centres have been erected throughout Britain during the last decade. In fact, the only good thing that may be said about unemployment is that it provides young people with more time to train, and ultimately produce better athletes. I must emphasize that this is not a state of affairs that I personally will accept, but I would agree that passing ones time engrossed in some form of sport is better than hanging around street corners.

But, enough of the serious stuff. Over the past three years or so, regular readers of local newspapers could hardly ignore the fact that the Gosport Borough Council seems to be placing great store in the future of leisure and pleasure, for much has appeared in print in connection with future projects in this field. Indeed, if all the ideas that have been mooted had materialized, the town would now be a veritable pleasure playground wallowing in a multitude of yachting marinas, ice-rinks, squash courts, golf courses, and even a magnificent 'Tropical Paradise' style swimming complex complete with potted palm trees and a simulated wave-machine! Thoughts of the latter immediately conjures visions of dusky maidens in grass skirts gyrating their pelvises and swaying their hips on the Gosport waterfront, and adorning disembarking visitors from the Portsmouth Ferry with garlands of flowers, this idyllic scene no doubt enhanced by the sight of the full Leisure Services Committee lined-up in the Ferry Gardens shouting "Aloha" to all and sundry!

However, I am afraid we shall have to cast our minds away from grass skirts and hula-hula dancing, and get back to sport. When I say get back to sport, I really do mean back, for although the town might be in the position to boast ice-rinks and suchlike in the future, my immediate concern is with the past. Since the far-off period that I shall be delving back to, sport has changed tremendously, and many older folk feel that it is far too commercially orientated now, thus encouraging a more ruthless approach to most sports. Their general opinion seems to be that when they played their particular sports, it was for the sake of the game. Anyway, in the following pages I hope to provide readers with a nostalgic, and light-hearted reminder of Gosport's sporting past, from football to billiards, and from bowls to hunting with the hounds.

Right, I think we are about ready for the off. Oh, excuse me just one moment, I must massage some Elliman's Athletic Rub into my wrinkled old kneecaps. Phew, what a pong! That stuff stills smells as pungently as it did forty years ago, a kind of cross between wintergreen and rotting seaweed! Okay, we are now under starter's orders. On Your Marks, Get Set, Go!

The victorious Gosport Albion side of 1921–22.

KICKING THE BALL AROUND

I think I would be correct in stating that football is the most popular game played in this country, for in my experience most male office and factory workers appear to devote some time on the Friday morning debating how the local team will fare in the match on Saturday, then on the following Monday they spend even more time discussing what went wrong, or perhaps what went right. It occurs to me that if the Russians invaded Cheltenham Spa over the weekend, or Sammy Davis Jnr. announced that he was going to marry Princess Margaret, the topic on Monday morning would still be whether Pompey will go up or down!

I must confess at this moment that I am not what one would describe an ardent football enthusiast, my chief concern with the game is in how many 3's I can get against the X's on my weekly coupon, and subsequently win enough money to keep up with the rate my family spend it. No, my interest in the actual game itself goes back to the days when players had their shorts way down below their knees, shirt sleeves buttoned at the wrists, and if a footballer did not sport a moustache, he was a sissy! The old players also had quaint habits, for if by chance they should knock an opponent off his feet, they would actually help them up, shake their hand and apologise most profusely. And another thing, there was not all this kissing and cuddling whenever a fellow player scored a goal, some of the players today act more like schoolgirls! Stop! Cancel that last remark, anyone who has observed schoolgirls playing hockey or netball will know that they play really rough! Too rugged for me anyway!

I shall in fact be dropping the odd word or so on ladies football teams in the area, but as it is essentially a male sport, we shall begin with the hairy-chested aspects of the game. So, come back with me to those balmy days around the turn of the century, when you could enjoy a great night out for only a couple of bob, and you could describe a chap as 'gay' without inviting curious glances.

In the annals of the Hampshire Football Association, Gosport figures very prominently, the Gosport and District League being the first junior league formed in the widespread area of the Portsmouth Football Association. Founded in the 1890's, the Gosport League owed much of its success in the early days to an enthusiast named Dan Mountifield. Although Dan worked hard on the administration side, being Hon. Secretary of the League for 21 years, in his younger days he was a player of some renown. He did in actual fact play for the Gosport Brightest Star club in 1894, then in 1896 he transferred to the Gosport Progressives, who could quite rightly claim to be one of the best sides on this side of the harbour during that period. It was a sad blow to local football when Dan Mountifield died in 1935 aged 60, but the League continued to flourish under the leadership of Frank Usher, another Gosport football stalwart who had been present at the birth of the League.

In the early years of this century the Gosport Progressives, who had been prominent in Portsmouth F.A. football, merged with the Gosport Athletics Sports Club as it's football section, and thus rose from the ranks of junior to senior football. At that time, the Athletic Club played their matches on public ground in Gosport Park, having to rely financially on collections taken whilst matches were in progress. Evidently, this method of raising funds was not too successful, and not enough money was passed via the hat to meet the expenses of their commitments in the Hampshire League, this meant that the football section had to draw heavily upon the general funds of the Sports Club. Eventually, matters came to a head when Gordon Park became available as a home pitch for the section, for the Sports Club could not guarantee to provide the heavier rent required. The football section decided to take the burden on its own shoulders, and established itself as Gosport United in 1903.

I am pleased to report that this venture proved successful, and Gosport United emerged as the town's most formidable team in the years prior to 1914. Being well into his 80's, my old friend George Foster has fond memories of United's progress during that period. I recall George telling me about one of the clubs star players, he was a Gosport solicitor named Thomas, and was known by local supporters as 'One-Eye Thomas'. Well, of course he only had one glass eye, it would have been a bit daft him playing football with two, wouldn't it? Anyway, during one particularly hectic game, the poor chap received a hefty knock and his glass eye fell out, resulting in the referee stopping the match whilst both teams joined in the search for the famous Thomas glass eye! I suppose you could say that this was not the first time that a player had not seen eye to eye with a referee!

Another early team to grace the local pitches was the famous Nyria Club, a side that made its name in the Gosport and Portsmouth Leagues, later developing into the Gosport Town Club. A large measure of the Nyria's success was due to the efforts of one of the towns most colourful characters, Sam Tomlinson. Through Sam's association with scouting in Gosport and the renowned 'Dive Cafe', regular readers of the 'Down Memory Lane' series will be aware that the name of Tomlinson has cropped up in almost every book about Gosport. Under Sam Tomlinson's guidance, Gosport Town Club maintained an excellent record, one of their greatest performances being when they held a prime Gosport Athletic Club side to a draw in the Hospital Cup, sadly losing the replay by three goals to one. Sam's association with both the Nyria and Town clubs extended over eighteen years, and at one time he was Vice-President of the Portsmouth Football Association. Gosport Town probably had their strongest line-up in 1920, this was when the squad included Garrett, Land, Odey, Keeping, Stainer, Lacey, Lockyer, Matheson, Staniland, Jackson, and Ginger Lewry wearing the badge of team captain.

Gosport in the 1980's has got quite a number of service bases in the area, mostly naval of course, but in the town of fifty to eighty years ago there was in addition a goodly number of army garrisons, plus a large flying establishment. Because of the facilities they were provided with, service teams were always exceptionally hard to beat, and generally hovered high in the local league tables. A succession of fine army teams passed through the gates of the New Barracks, the King's Own Light Infantry and the King's Royal Rifles being but two examples. The 4th Company R.E. based at Fort Monckton could also be relied upon to provide tough opposition, even against the famous 15th Company Royal Artillery. Coming to the fore in the 1890's, the 15th Company were absolute dynamite, generally sweeping all before them under the leadership of their trainer, Sergeant Morgan. In 1894 they amalgamated with their closest rivals, the Depot R.A., and this was akin to Arsenal joining forces with Tottenham Hotspur, a dynamic duo indeed. Led by Sergeant Bonney, they won almost every local competition in sight, and in 1896 they reached the final of the English Amateur Cup, narrowly beaten 1–0 by Bishop Auckland. The Royal Garrison Artillery when stationed at Fort Brockhurst also struck fear into the hearts of local teams in Gosport, and their transfer to Woolwich in 1921 probably brought sighs of relief from some quarters. But before their departure, they had the pleasure of

First Gosport Athletic Team 1919.

Priddy's Hard F.C. 1913.

Clarence Athletic F.C. 1923.

Gosport 'Nyria's', 1909.
Sam Tomlinson seated in centre.

The outstanding R.M.L.I. team of 1910.

beating the R.M.L.I. 3–0 to win the coveted Victory Cup.

Mention of the R.M.L.I., Royal Marine Light Infantry, reminds us of those marvellous years when they were based at Forton Barracks. Many marines stationed at Forton married local girls, and living in Gosport it was like being with one big happy family, so it stands to reason that the sporting prowess of the R.M.L.I. was followed keenly. Their fortunes were at their highest in 1910, and what a year that was for them. Their first success was at Aldershot where they fought hard to beat the 1st. Bat. Royal Irish Fusiliers 2–0, thus winning the coveted Army Cup. The good news was immediately phoned through to Forton, whereupon the Commandant ordered men to race around the town on their bicycles in order to rally the various bandsmen who resided in the area. This resulted in the victorious R.M.L.I. team being met at Gosport Railway Station with a rousing reception, complete with a band and hundreds of cheering townsfolk. As they marched in triumph to Forton Barracks, they were followed by swarms of local lads, and George Foster was right there with them all the way. George recalls the occasion well, for it resulted in him arriving home late, and his father taking off his belt to him. This incident was not helped by the fact that George's father was a Navy man and supporter, and did not take kindly to the Marine's great success.

But, a few weeks later the Forton folk had an even greater success to celebrate, for the R.M.L.I. team went to Bishop Auckland and beat South Bank by two goals to one to win the F.A. Amateur Cup. The people of Gosport went crackers when the news was received, and children ran through the streets chanting: "Hurrah! The Lillywhites have won, they beat poor old South Bank by two goals to one!". When the team returned to the town, the reception was even greater than before, a tram was taken over at the Hard and the players stood waving on the top deck to a sea of people. They had with them their team mascot, an elderly gent named Bryan who had a wooden leg. In the excitement his peg-leg was unscrewed and a Union Jack affixed to it, then it was secured to the front of the tram for all to see. My goodness, what a magnificent boost for Gosport that must have been, I am afraid that it is unlikely that such as occasion will happen again, although we can live in hopes!

Before we discard our uniforms, I would remind readers that many star footballers emerged from service teams to join professional clubs in the days when the game was just beginning to make an impact. The aforementioned R.A.'s provided several gifted players, one of them being the great Matt Reilly, goalkeeper extraordinary. Matt was actually a member of the very first 'Pompey' team in 1899, and thanks to his safe hands they finished their first season with second place in the Southern League, being runners-up to Spurs.

Meanwhile, back in dear old Gosport, the pitches in Gordon Park were deteriorating rapidly. Several old players have told me how bad facilities were in those days, especially when they had to try and wash the mud off at the end of a game, they had to make do with a smoke belching old boiler which had seen better days. But, even this was an improvement on the pre-1914 days when Gosport United played there regularly, when there were no changing rooms at all. Eventually, the landlord of the nearby 'Gipsy Queen' came to their rescue, and teams were allowed to change in the pub. The crunch finally came when Gordon Park was acquired by the Gosport Education Committee after the First World War, so football supporters had to find a new venue, and a move was made to Bury Park in The Avenue.

The mention of education in the last paragraph, reminds us that local schools played an important role in the history of the game in the town, providing several young players who went on to make their mark in football. There was certainly great rivalry between the various school teams, and matches between

Clarence Square Boys and Newtown Boys were always well worth watching. The lads generally fought for trophies such as the Brodrick Cup, or the Blake Shield. But, whoever won or lost, there was always a huge beanfeast at the 'Royal Arms' for the two teams reaching the final. The lads were entertained by landlord Jim Smith in a large tent erected in the yard at the rear of the pub, and it was a case of lemonade and sticky cakes all round. Our Jim was a great football enthusiast, in fact he loved most sports, and could rightly claim to be one of the few non-drinking publicans in the town.

During his academic career, Frank Small taught at both Newtown and Clarence Square schools, and he did a great deal to pioneer schoolboy football in the area. Frank could not only talk football, he could play it with considerable skill, playing for some of the best teams in the local leagues, including Gosport Town. And of course, I must mention two other renowned footballing teachers, Arthur Sherwin and Geoff Civil, both tricky players to tackle in their time. The last time that I spoke to Frank Small, just before he died in 1981 at the age of 90, he could still remember that marvellous Brodrick Cup Final in 1925 between Newtown Boys and Clarence Square. It was such a good match, it was a shame that there had to be losers, but on that occasion Newton emerged as the victors by one goal to nil. The winning team comprised Reed, Gasser, Day, Robins, Churcher, Wagstaff, Jenkins, Wey, Keech, Cantle, and Webb was captain. Yes, it was a proud moment for the 'Cherry Stripes', and nobody was prouder than headmaster Mr. Gregory and masters Mr. Germain and Mr. Smith. However, there was some consolation for the Clarence Square Boys, that year they won the Blake Shield.

Around that period in time Newtown could boast a brilliant young goalkeeper named Doug Preston, and in 1926 he was chosen to play for the England Youth Team, his first Interna-tional being against Scotland. Following his excellent debut, Doug turned out for England on several other occasions. Clarence Square School also had a budding young footballer who was destined to reach international status, but of course, nobody realised it at the time. Wally Barnes had his football apprenticeship in the local school and district leagues, and in addition to his obvious skills with the ball, he was also very useful in the boxing ring. Wally was actually born in Brecon, home of the South Wales Borderers, his father being a provost sergeant in that famous regiment. When he was five years old the family went out to India for four years, returning when he was nine to take up residence in Gosport. As he got older his footballing skills were soon revealed, in fact he was good enough to be put on the books of Portsmouth F.C. as an amateur. During this period in his career, Pompey were due to play a friendly match against Southampton, but there was not room for Wally in the team, so he turned out for a weakened Saints side against his own club. It was all rather embarrassing really, for Saints beat Pompey by three goals to nil. Now, just guess who scored all three goals? That is right, young Wally Barnes! The rest of course is history, he went on to play as a pro for Southampton, and subsequently for Arsenal, where I had the pleasure of watching him play in the immediate post-war years. Although both his parents were Londoners, as he was born in Wales he was eligible to play for that country, and donned the international shirt for them many times. After his retirement from the game, and up until his untimely death, Wally gained great respect as a broadcaster and football pundit.

Although it is rather glamorous dropping names such as Saints, Pompey, and Wales, we must return to the Gosport football scene. After the 1914–18 war, the Gosport Albion were one of the foremost teams to attract supporters within the town. The Albion developed from the former Brodrick Athletic Club,

St. John's Old Boys F.C. 1920–21.
Winners of Gosport League Div. II.

The great Newtown side of 1925–26.

and many of their players originated from Alverstoke School. Albion had a talented centre-forward in the shape of Tom Gorman, a real sharp-shooter. His two brothers also played in the team, Reg in the inside-right position, whilst Bert at outside-left provided the centres for brother Tom. Most followers of this side in those days were of the opinion that although Tom Gorman was a heck of a shot and stole all the glory, they were in no doubt that brother Reg was the better ball player. Still, what did it matter as long as they won, and win they did, their best seasons being in the early 20's. In the 1921–22 season Albion won the First Division Championship of the Gosport and District League, as well as the Portsmouth Junior Cup. In the following season they won the league again, plus the Senior Hospital Cup. In fact, in that 1922–23 season they were unbeaten, and their supporters could not complain about lack of goals, for Albion scored a total of 140. I would add that out of this huge number of goals in one season, Tom Gorman scored 85 of them. Wow, many of our top teams today would like 85 goals to their credit, let alone one player. In 1929, Tom Gorman scored six goals for England in an amateur trial game at Northampton, he was also at one time on the books of Southampton and Chelsea.

Win or lose, the Gosport Albion Club always appeared ready to celebrate at their headquarters, the Park Hotel in Alverstoke. They would get the official business over as soon as possible, then Miss Lester would leap up onto the piano stool whilst the Club President, Mr. Rowland, led a riotous sing-song! Thanks to my old chum Dave Gasser, I have in my possession a Gosport Albion Members Card for the season 1923–24, and it is absolutely packed with useful information. Mr. S. Hunt was the President for that year, but the list of Vice-Presidents reads like a Gosport Who's Who, including Alderman John Windebank, Councillor J. Jones, George Wall, Peter Tostevin, Fred Salter,

Sam Tomlinson, and R.T. House Esq., amongst others. That particular year they had their headquarters at The Vine in Stoke Road, and their home ground was Gordon Park. A great cheer always went up when the Gosport Albion ran onto the pitch in their strip of maroon jerseys and white shorts, with their trainers in close attendance, the latter including Alf Poore, Charlie Standhaft, and Reg Geary. But, all good things must come to an end, and it could be said that too much success killed the Gosport Albion Club. They worked their way up from junior football to the championship of the Hants League Eastern Division, and in 1927 they went into the County League Competition, but unfortunately after a short period they found that their finances could not stand the strain, and they eventually made an application to withdraw.

If the game of football has changed tremendously over the years, then I guess crowd behaviour has changed considerably also, the modern trend of violence on the terraces springing immediately to mind. Mind you, I do not profess that the football fans of yesteryear were exactly angels, but their verbal dialogue was conducted more on the lines of good natured heckling, rather than abuse of the nasty kind. Positioned closer to their audience, wingers generally took the brunt from sarcastic comments, such as: "Cor, you call that a pass, I've seen better centres in a box of Black Magic". And of course, the poor old referees have always had their fair share of heckling from spectators: "I say Ref, shouldn't you be wearing a pair of ****** glasses". I don't know about wearing spectacles, I feel referees might be better off wearing ear plugs. They did not take kindly to bad language in days gone by, especially from players in the course of a game. During one local match back in 1920 concerning the formidable Grange R.A.F. team, one of their star players resorted to swearing behind the back of the ref. Unfortunately for him, the official had good hearing, and sent him off. The player was subsequently suspended for several vital forthcoming matches, and during an appeal that followed before a committee of league officials, it was stated on his behalf that he had a habit of speaking his thoughts out loud! The appeal fell upon deaf ears!

It turned out to be quite a rough affair during a match in 1919 in which R.N. Ordnance played against Gosport Wesleyans who were leading 1–0, so the R.N.O. resorted to playing the dirty stuff, accompanied by suitable language. Their goalkeeper was the worst, and displayed his temper by kicking the ball over the sea wall. The ref gave him a warning, but ten minutes later the goalie kicked a second ball out to sea. The ref had had enough, and asked the R.N.O.'s captain the name of his goalkeeper, but the captain refused to give it. At this moment the offensive goalkeeper decided to kick another ball over the sea wall! That was it, they only had three balls, so the game was abandoned seven minutes before the end. An appeal was held later, and the Wesleyan team were awarded the league points. So, what was the name of the goalkeeper? I can reveal that it was Garrett, but don't tell the referee! One way or another, it was a pretty hazardous business playing football in the Haslar area, for on more than one occasion it was not only the ball that ended up in the sea, several players also went home in wet gear. However, there was one attack that the footballers at Haslar did not bargain for, from the air. This happened in the 1930's when a Spartan Cruiser aircraft belonging to Allied British Airways ran out of fuel and had to make a forced landing at Haslar. With the pilot struggling at the controls, the plane hurtled down towards the startled footballers, and needless to say, they in turn proceeded to give very good impressions of moles by trying to tunnel under the pitch. By a miracle, the aircraft cleared the prone bodies and was eventually brought to a stop by crashing through the hedge of a garden attached to the residence of Colonel Downs. The players gathered their wits and ran over to the wreckage of the plane, only to be met by the pilot climbing out of the cabin and calmly announcing: "Hello chaps, I am sorry if I gave you a scare".

Although football was generally encouraged in most Gosport schools, many residents of the town strongly objected to lads playing in the streets, especially those who had a ball kicked through the windows of their front parlours. Feelings ran high, with a result that many boys were brought before the local magistrates and actually fined for kicking a ball in a built-up area. Thank goodness there were a number of public spirited folk around to do something more tangible to solve the problem, they formed small clubs in order to keep the youngsters off of the streets. In 1914, Gosport had a very good youth team in the form of the Gosport Minors F.C., who later changed their name to Gosport Jacquoer F.C. Mr. Roy Gunton was the driving force behind this very successful club.

Gosport United had represented the town before the First World War, but when the war was over there appeared to be little enthusiasm for a revival. As a vacancy was left in the Portsmouth League, it was felt that a new Gosport club would be required. Following an inspired meeting at the Royal Arms, hosted by our old friend Jim Smith and kept in order by Ben Kent in the chairman's seat, a new team did indeed run out onto the Gosport football pitches in 1919, enter Gosport Athletic. Within a short space of time, Athletic established themselves as Gosport's premier team, and were able to boast of having in their midst some of the finest footballers in the South of England. The late Reg Gardner was a member of the very first Athletic team in 1919, and stayed on to see them through their most successful seasons, notably 1923–24 when they finished by winning three cups, the Portsmouth Senior Cup, the Hospital Cup, and the Hampshire League Championship. Reg Gardner

The famous "Hardway Vic's" 1921.

Christ Church F.C. 1909–10.

Brodrick Cup Finalists, Clarence Square. Wally Barnes on the right of kneeling goalkeeper in front.

Gosport Town F.C. 1919.

C & N Football Team 1951–52.

was also chosen to play for the Hampshire County side, and wore that shirt with distinction several times. Although he died in February 1983 at the age of 84, having played an important part in Gosport's sporting past, I sincerely trust that through this modest publication the name of Reg Gardner will be remembered for some time to come.

But, Gosport Athletic had so many talented players, chaps such as Harry Tutt, Monty McCullen, Bert Patter, Bill Pacey, Geoff Civil, Neil, Wiggins, Lewis, Bennett, Woolard, Yendall, Ayling, Robinson, and Cyril Hennen. Cyril played for Athletic before crossing the Solent to play for Ryde, another fine Southern team. He returned to Gosport later for a spell with Gosport Albion, and just to add insult to injury, he helped Albion beat his old club Ryde 1–0 in the Portsmouth Divisional Cup.

Bill Pacey was always a great favourite with Gosport Athletic supporters, for they could always be sure of plenty of action when big Bill was playing. He was what one would term a robust player, and if he was not involved or booked in a skirmish, the fans would deem that they had not had their monies worth. During one very important cup match at Forton, Bill was ordered by the ref to leave the pitch, a decision that was regarded as unfair by his fellow Athletic players. Skipper Perce Neil felt so strongly about it he marched his team off of the field, and they did not return! Bill Pacey was still playing football when he was in his 40's, turning out for the Gas Company team in his latter years. He was in the team when he was the oldest player, and Wally Barnes was the youngest. Bill died in 1974 aged 79, another sportsman who rates high on the Gosport Sporting Roll of Fame.

In their halcyon years Gosport Athletic were fortunate in having the services of Mr. J.L. Fleming as their secretary, for he was much respected for his official work for the Hampshire Football Association. As a pupil at Leesland School he learnt his football during the dinner hours on the adjacent brickfield, then in 1903 he joined the old Gosport Victorias F.C., later taking over as secretary as well as playing. The Victorias finished high in the Portsmouth Lads' League in the 1910–11 season, and from 1911 to 1914 they were members of the Second Division of the Gosport and District Football League. During the war the club remained dormant, and although it was revived in 1919, the Victorias eventually disbanded in 1923 because many of the members were forced to leave Gosport due to the prevailing unemployment situation. Mr. Fleming had much to do with the success of the Armament Supply Depot team before taking over as secretary of Gosport Athletic in 1924.

I have mentioned previously that the 1923–24 season was a great one for Athletic, and I would add that they also enjoyed a good run in the F.A. Cup that year. They went to Weymouth for a cliff-hanging match that ended with two goals apiece, so needless to say there was a large crowd at Bury Park for the replay. Weymouth were leading 1–0 at half-time, but Ayling equalised in the second half with a penalty, so it was another draw. The second replay was held at the Dean Court ground in Bournemouth, and although the Gosport team fought hard, at the closing whistle they had lost by three goals to nil. The score would have been greater if it had been for the brilliant saving of Trapp, the Athletic goalkeeper. Gosport fans had a small measure of revenge a few weeks later, for Gosport Boys beat Weymouth Boys 6–0 in the English Schools Shield.

Several Gosport Athletic players turned professional, and it is only natural that because of the towns close proximity to Portsmouth some of them joined the Pompey squad, in fact Gosport has a worthy record over the past sixty years for supplying players for Fratton Park. Athletic provided talents such as Len Gill, Ginger Lewry, and Bibby Edwards amongst

"Brodrick Cup" finalists 1931.

Gosport Albion 1922–23.
Tom Gorman holding ball.

The renowned Brodrick's F.C.

Ray Hiron.
Gosport F.C. & Portsmouth F.C.
Photo J.C. Lawrence.

others. Edwards got his big break through another players misfortune, he was playing well with the Pompey Reserves and adding to his goal tally quite consistently, then Jerry Mackie had to drop out of the first team and return home through the death of his mother. Bibby was immediately brought in to make his first team debut against Saints, and from that moment he never looked back.

Two other Gosport Athletic stalwarts that we must not neglect come in the shapes of Ginger Stafford and Jack Gray. Ginger was the teams first goalkeeper, and standing between the posts with his six foot two inches it is understandable that not too many balls got past him. Jack Gray was a legend in local football and in the county, for he was chief trainer to the Athletic and also County XI trainer for many years, and if one scans photographs of past Hampshire representative teams it is amazing how many times the familiar cloth-capped figure of Jack Gray appears.

Before I blow the final whistle on Gosport Athletic, I simply must mention a man who has devoted a lifetime to the game, both as a player and as an official, I refer of course to Stan Cribb. As far as Gosport is concerned, Stan just has to be the towns Mister Football, for his association with soccer includes both the amateur and professional game, and even in his 80's he still has strong ties with the sport. Stan Cribb learnt his Three R's at Grove Road School, this was when Mr. Jordan was the headmaster there. I must add that Grove Road was another Gosport school that did sterling work in the early days to encourage boys to work off their surplus energy by playing football. Anyhow, it was obvious that as a youngster Stan was blessed with footballing skills, so it is not surprising that as he got older he should progress into the crack Gosport Athletic side. He was in the Athletic team for that wonderful 1923–24 season, and although he was the youngest player amidst seasoned veterans, he played in every one of the clubs 54 games during that period. Athletic finished the season with 154 goals to their credit, of which young Cribb had scored 14. This was highly creditable, for in a team that could boast such prolific goal-scorers as Lewry, Robinson, and Edwards, I should think that it was difficult to find a spare space anywhere near the opposing goal area.

That could well have been Athletic's greatest season, but for Stan Cribb it was just the beginning, for he had been spotted as a bright prospect for pro football. In 1924 he signed for Southampton F.C., this was when the maximum fee for a professional player was £8 a week during the season, and £6 a week in the summer break. This may appear awfully low by todays standards, but I can assure readers that it was a good wage at a time when the average was under three quid a week. Stan had hardly got his Southampton shirt muddy when he had to play for them against his old side in a friendly match. That was one match that Trapp the Athletic goalie would have been pleased to forget, for the Saints put six balls past him into the back of the net.

Stan Cribb remained with Southampton until 1931, and remembers them as very happy days. From The Dell, he moved to London to join West Ham for a season, then in 1933 he transferred to Queens Park Rangers. During his spell with Q.P.R. he set a record for a winger in first-class football by scoring 19 goals in twelve consecutive matches, a record that I believe still stands. His next move took him to Wales, where he played for Cardiff City. Unfortunately, it was during his time there that he sustained a very bad knee injury that was to put him out of the game, thus ending the professional playing career of a man who was reputed to be the hardest dead-ball kicker in pro football, and the scourge of goalkeepers when taking penalties.

But, that was not the end of Stan's interest in the game, for he

Haslar Sports F.C. League winners 1943–44.
Stan Cribb standing extreme left.
Eddie Crossland is goalkeeper.

St. Faith's F.C. 1921–22.

Gosport Gas Company F.C. 1930's.
Bill Pacey seated 3rd. from right.

St. Faith's Second XI. 1922–23.

Bury Park crowd at 1923 Cup-tie.
Gosport Athletic v. Weymouth.

returned to Gosport, where with Councillor Alf Eales he helped to form Gosport Borough Athletic in 1944. Stan was in fact appointed manager of the Borough, and remained in that position for 23 years, his service being recognised by the presentation of a silver tea service. The Supporters Club were also very aware of his good work, and they gave Stan a chiming mantle clock and wrist watches for his wife and himself, momentos that he treasures. Stan's two great loves in the game have been Gosport Borough and Southampton F.C., and he has retained his connection with Saints in his capacity as youth talent scout. After all, with his wide experience, who could recognize young footballing talent better than Stan?

Despite Gosport Athletic's great success, by 1925 it was found that the clubs financial position was not in very good shape, and it proved to be a worrying time for the Chairman Mr. W. Harding, the Treasurer Mr. A. Benham, and Mr. J. Fleming the Secretary. They managed to carry on for a few years, but by 1928 they were experiencing the same difficulties as Gosport Albion. Not the sort of chap to let the grass grow under his feet, the Mayor of Gosport at that time, Alderman Ben Kent, called a public meeting with a view to uniting Albion and Athletic to form a new team that would continue under the name of Gosport Football Club. Whatever Ben Kent said was generally accepted as making good sense, so he was elected as President of the club, and Gosport now possessed a team that had a combination of some of the best footballing talents in the area.

And so, the new Gosport F.C. ran onto the pitch for the first time to open the 1928–29 season, resplendent in their outfits of white shorts and blue and yellow shirts with the Borough Arms on the chest. That first match at Bury Park was a friendly against Pompey, and it attracted over 2,000 spectators. Punch White had a marvellous game in goal, saving several hard shots from the pro players, and Gosport did well to hold the visitors to a 3–3 draw. After the match, all the players and officials retired to the Swiss Cafe in the High Street for a good beano, thanks to the hospitality of Ben Kent. Ben really was a most remarkable character, and thoroughly deserved the title afforded to him as The Sporting Mayor. Born in the West Country in the 1860's, he moved to Gosport through his work in 1886, bringing with him his love of sport. He had previously played rugby for Devon Albions, a very famous team in the 1880's, then on his move to this area he played for Portsmouth Albion and Portsmouth Town. Strangely enough, although he never played Association Football, he became recognised as one of the best judges of the game, and he served the Hampshire Football Association for over 25 years. He was at one time the Vice-President of the County Association, and he was also hon. secretary of the Portsmouth Football Association.

The fortunes of Gosport F.C. fluctuated in the years leading up to the Second World War, one of their happiest seasons being in 1934 when they won the Russell-Cotes Cup and were runners-up in the County League, whilst one of their unhappiest moments was in 1936 when they were beaten by Dulwich in the Amateur Cup by eleven goals to nil! Still, 1937 was a year for the Gosport Club to remember, for they at long last gained a new home at Privett Park. Thanks to the enterprise of Gosport Borough Council, and a gentle nudging from Ben Kent, the players and supporters could enjoy much-improved accommodation and facilities. The enclosed ground comprised a railed-off pitch and a stand capable of seating 600, with de-luxe dressing rooms below for the players. The ground really was quite unique for that period, and for many visiting teams it was akin to coming to Wembley. The ground was formally opened by the Mayor, Alderman Charles Graham, on Wednesday 1st September. He did this by throwing the first ball into the new arena, thus opening a match between Gosport F.C. and Ryde F.C. Gosport fielded a strong team in the form of Feast, Lockyer, Giles, Blackwell, Baker, Williams, Davies, O'Harrow, Brickwood, Dawe and Stevenson. Unfortunately, they were not strong enough, for Ryde beat them 4–2, thus bringing a cloud to what had otherwise been a momentous occasion in the history of the Gosport club. I might add that the late Ernie Ramage was playing for Ryde at that time, he had previously played for Gosport. Ernie was a talented inside-right with a flair for coming up trumps when the chips were down, and made several appearances for the Hants County XI. I had the pleasure of having Ernie as a working colleague for many years, and I will never forget his ever-smiling face.

As mentioned previously, after the war the club flourished under the guidance of Stan Cribb, and in the ensuing thirty years or so have experienced both triumph and disappointment. They have also provided Pompey and other professional clubs with several talented players, Ray Hiron and Gary Juryeff being but two examples. I have not enough space to mention all the players who remained loyal and served Gosport Borough well, but I must devote a couple of lines to veteran Bud Fisher, whom followers may recall from the early 50's. Bud was almost indestructible, and during his long service I should think that he played in every position on the field, including that of goalkeeper. Bringing the story up-to-date, Gosport Borough F.C. are playing in the Premier Division of the Southern League, and like many other clubs around the country, they have their share of financial problems. Still, we must hope that the position will improve, it would be a tragedy if a town the size of Gosport did not have a football side to represent it.

At the beginning of this section I promised a few lines on ladies football in Gosport, and although many chaps think it is manly to play football, I think that it is even more manly to watch ladies playing football! Work that one out! I am pleased to

Stan Cribb in Q.P.R. days. 1933.

24

Gosport Athletic Veterans Team.
Including Hennen – Lewry – Gardner – Cribb – Pacey.

Alverstoke Ladies F.C. 1919.

Hants and Dorset Ladies Team 1942.

Priddy's Hard Ladies Team 1917–18.

Southdown and Provincial Teams at Privett Park.

George Tomlinson seated in the middle of this glamorous group. Sam Tomlinson on extreme right.

Brockhurst Cricket Club 1927.

say that at the present time we have several ladies football leagues dotted around the country, and I look forward to the future when the 'equality for women' brigade campaign for 'mixed' football, men and women playing together. The prospect of this almost has me leaping into the loft to find my old Stanley Matthews Mk. III football boots, and I know one thing for sure, I would never complain about the aforementioned practice of kissing and cuddling when a goal is scored, or about swapping shirts with opponents at the end of a game!

Sam Tomlinson introduced ladies football matches to the town. It all began as a charity event for fund-raising in the 1914–18 war, with a Gosport side coached by Sam playing against a Portsmouth ladies side organized by Mr. Hammond. I believe that the Gosport girls emerged as the winners, but regardless of the result, not too many legs were bitten or very much hair pulled from heads, and the event raised £50 for the funds of the forthcoming War Memorial Hospital. It is interesting to recall that this first ladies team to represent Gosport was recruited from the ammunition factory at Priddy's Hard. Whilst playing football, the girls actually wore the cute little mop hats that they wore when working. Eventually, the cordite that they worked with made their hair go ginger, hence the protective caps. I should think that the last thing to worry about when working in an ammunition factory was having your hair go ginger, which in turn reminds me of a newspaper advert that read: "Young man required for Dynamite Factory–Must be willing to travel".

The success of this venture inspired Sam Tomlinson to arrange further games, and assisted by his son George, the two of them ensured that Christmas Day Ladies Football Matches became a regular event on the Gosport calendar. There was never any shortage of female footballing talent to call upon, for many ladies crewed on the local trams and buses in those days, and the

Tomlinson's 'Dive Cafe' happened to be a popular venue for transport folk. Many of the all-ladies matches took place between Provincial Girls and Hants & Dorset Girls, they were always well supported, and generally produced a glut of unusual goals.

I have just been struck with an impish thought. If ladies football really became popular in this country, think how it would revolutionize the game. I am intrigued by the advertising aspect for one thing, just imagine it, no longer would we have those manly adverts proclaiming the wonders of Brylcream, or Gillette Razor Blades, these could be replaced by showboards for Max Factor's Eye Shadow, or Sunsilk Hairspray. I can see it now, a hoarding on the side of a pitch advising fans about the advantages of wearing a Cross-Your-Heart Bra! Well, at least that is one way of getting supporters! This could also raise questions regarding that great hairy-chested footballer with the word 'Mum' tattooed on his equally hairy arm. Is he really advertising a well-known deodorant?

Oh well, you can now take off your football boots, a quick rub-down and a slice of lemon, and we will be on our way to the next sporting event.

KNOCKING THE BALL AROUND

I trust that everybody has taken off their football boots by now, for we are ready to look back at other ways of striking a ball. This section will cover sports that require a piece of equipment of some kind to manipulate a ball, and it is quite surprising how many games fall into this category. I cannot possibly touch upon them all, but I shall endeavour to include the most popular.

When I think of cricket, I immediately conjure a vision of a village green adorned by gentlemen in dazzling white, with spectators lounging outside a wooden pavilion in deckchairs, sipping tea and joining in with the occasional ripples of polite applause. If a ball should pass over the boundary line, the onlookers are liable to increase the volume of their hand-clapping, and may even offer an enthusiastic: "Well done, old chap". Yes, the game of cricket just has to be the most English of English institutions.

My favourite cricket story concerns Harold Larwood, the great England fast bowler of the pre-war years. During one match, Harold sent down a ferocious ball that struck the batsman's pad long before he could get his bat to it. Turning to the umpire, the fast bowler cried "Owzat?". The umpire did not bat an eyelid. Harold hurtled down another ball, and once again it beat the bat to strike the leg pad. Another appeal went up, but the umpire still did not flinch. Taking an even longer run, the bowler sent down the ball like an express train, the batsman never even saw it, the stumps were knocked out of the ground and the bails disappeared into the great blue yonder! Harold looked at the umpire and said: "Phew, I was close that time!".

In the early days of cricket, it was definitely a game for the upper crust, and was mostly indulged in by naval and military gentlemen. As the Gosport of yesteryear abounded in military establishments, it was only natural that cricket should be popular in this area, and like prize-fighting in those days, it attracted a fair amount of side-betting. The stakes did not always concern money, I have a report of a cricket match that took place locally in 1834 in which Five Gentlemen of Haslar played against Five Gentlemen of Gosport on the Camp Ground, the prize for the winners being a 'rump and dozen'. I am sorry, I have no idea which side won.

The cricket lovers of Gosport have Colonel Charles Mumby to thank for putting the game on a more permanent footing in the town, this being in the latter years of the last century. Gosport had an excellent cricket club then, and due to Colonel Mumby's initiative they were able to play on a well maintained pitch in the centre of the Horsefield. Unfortunately, when the local authority entered into an agreement with the Admiralty to lease the ground, the cricket club lost their pitch. But, the Colonel came to their rescue again, setting his eyes on the area known as Ewer Common, and with the possibilities of using it not only for cricket, but also for other recreational pursuits. With the help of Major Appleby from Fareham, Colonel Mumby entered into negotiations with the owners of the land, the Ecclesiastical Commissioners. Eventually, the land was handed over on the condition that it was made perfectly free for the use of the public. The cost of acquiring the land was less that £100, I hate to think what it would be worth today. Nine acres were laid out for cricket, thus maintaining a local interest in the game, and the grand opening of Gosport park took place in the June of 1891, with local dignitries and general public alike doing their best to make it into a festive occasion. In addition to the many bright

Gosport Gas Company C.C. 1929.

The outstanding Gosport Borough C.C.
that went to Lords in 1980.

and colourful stalls, the side-shows and a resplendent military band in attendance, the highlight of the afternoon was to be a cricket match between members of the Portsmouth Town Council and the Gosport Public Bodies. Led by former Mayor Sir William King in a splendid carriage, the visitors made a grand entrance into the new park. This imposing cavalcade appears to have impressed the public men of Gosport so much, they never got over their awe for the opposition and were well beaten in the ensuing cricket match.

Despite this defeat, the cricketers of Gosport were not dejected, and from that moment the sport really took off in the town. Several sides emerged from local industrial and commercial concerns, and the game was also adopted by football clubs in order that their players should keep fairly fit throughout the summer months. Most of the prominent clubs in Gosport had a cricket section, and there was no shortage of sides to fill the leagues of the Gosport & District Cricket Association. Most of the fixtures were played on Sunday afternoons or on weekday evenings, there was even a league on Wednesday afternoons for half-day shop workers.

Bringing our cricket story to more recent times, in the 50's and early 60's the most prominent clubs were those of the Gosport Cricket Club and the Gosport Amateurs. Then, in 1966, the two clubs merged to form Gosport Borough Cricket Club, rather similar to the football amalgamation that ultimately led to the forming of Gosport Borough F.C. When one studies the local cricket scene over the past twenty years, it becomes apparent that it is very much a family sport, with sons following in their fathers footsteps, or perhaps 'run-ups' would be a more appropriate term. One of the family names that stands out in the history of the Gosport Borough C.C. is that of Farley, well known locally for their printing business on Fareham's Wickham Road. Tim Farley has been President of the Borough C.C. since

1981, this following his service as Club Chairman. His two sons, Peter and Ian, have also enjoyed successes in the sport. Formerly playing for Gosport, Ian now straps on pads for the fine Waterlooville team that graces the Town & Country Southern Cricket League. Gosport Borough C.C. also manage to finish most seasons fairly high in the same league, led by Captain Peter Farley. In the 1970's, Peter enjoyed a number of great cricketing experiences out in Australia, where he played with and against some of that country's most formidable players, the list includes Dennis Lillee, Ross Edwards, Rodney Marsh, Jim Hubble, and Graeme McKenzie.

Over the years, Gosport has produced several players who were talented enough to join the Hampshire County C.C., and amongst this select band we must of course include Trevor Jesty. This fine all-rounder played for Gosport Cricket Club as a youth, and some local followers of the game may remember his brother, Aubrey Jesty, who played for Gosport Amateurs in the pre-merger days. The bowling skills of Alan Wassell have also been good enough to get him a place in the Hampshire team, in fact he was in their Championship-winning side of a few years ago. Alan still plays for the Borough side, and in his long service with them has taken a remarkable 1,353 wickets to date, this figure including 82 matches in which he has taken 5 wickets. His son, John Wassell, has also made his mark for Borough C.C. Another father and son combination is that of Jim and Tony Stares, and both have notched-up fine records for the club. His batting and bowling figures show only too well Jim's prowess as an all-rounder, he has hit 5,520 runs, and taken 884 wickets. Ray Porter is another Gosport player who has not been dozing in the outfield, his skills as an all-rounder has gained him 6,878 runs, and given him 801 wickets. But, the award for the most swashbuckling player must go to big-hitter Mick Swain, who has been the scourge of bowlers and a headache to score-board operators with his fantastic tally of 12,500 runs. This figure includes 15 centuries, and 74 fifties.

There is no doubt about which was the finest moment in the history of the Gosport Borough C.C., it just has to be that magnificent season in 1980 when they fought their way to the final of the John Haig National Club Cricket Championship at Lords. If anyone has any doubts about this as an achievement, let them reflect that the finalists are gradually whittled down from some 500 clubs throughout the country. The great match took place on Saturday the 23rd of August in 1980, and what a marvellous moment it must have been for Captain Peter Farley and his team as they strolled out onto the revered turf of Lords. Sadly, they lost the final against Mosley, but it did not detract from the achievement of actually getting there, a magnificent feat in itself. The Gosport club still attracts many followers, and home fixtures at Privett Park are always well worth a visit. Finally, before washing the linseed oil off my hands, I must mention the current Chairman, Derek Barrett, and Doug Scorey, the hard working Secretary and Treasurer of the Gosport C.C. I might also add that Farleys' sponsor the South Hampshire Indoor Cricket League, the matches are played at the Fleming Park Sports Centre at Eastleigh, and at the time of writing the Gosport Borough side look like winning the championship yet again.

Right, what else can we hit a ball with? How about hockey? Although this game is usually associated with schoolgirls, it is one of the roughest, toughest sports that one can play. I played for a while when I was in the Army, and I cannot recall one match in which at least one of my fellow players did not get away without injury. We dreaded playing Indian teams when abroad, they always ran rings around us. Still, I am pleased that we did not have to take on a team like St. Trinian's, even the Indians would have shuddered at such a prospect!

Once again, hockey is another sport that was adopted readily by the services, although over the years there have been a number of good local teams. One of the more unusual teams hit the local hockey scene at the latter end of the Second World War, known as the 'Brockhurst Dodgers', the group was formed by teenagers who had learnt their hockey in local schools. The youngsters endeavoured to run two teams as cheaply as they were able, paying sixpence per match each in order to keep funds flowing for pitch fees and a supply of balls. They even played in a strip of all-white, not being able to afford expensive kit. They liked playing service teams, because such sides tended to be rather careless about looking after their supply of hockey balls! To avoid argument in selecting teams, the Dodgers squad only comprised eleven men and five women. The men played mens hockey on Saturdays, then six of them joined the ladies for mixed hockey on Sundays. Kenneth Harrison, who was secretary of the club at that time, assures me that mixed hockey was by far the roughest and most dangerous activity.

Strangely enough, from this motley crew there emerged several players who were on the fringe of County recognition, and although they played for the sheer fun of it, the Brockhurst Dodgers defeated some of the most powerful clubs on the local hockey scene, even when they were not able to field a full team, sometimes playing as many as three short. But, like all good things, it had to end, and eventually the demands of courting and conscription made it difficult to keep going. The remaining players were readily accepted by the Hockey Section of Gosport Borough Athletic Club, and the Brockhurst Dodgers graced the local pitches no longer. However, former members such as Ken Harrison still retain fond memories of the club's days of glory.

Anyone for tennis? I must admit that I do not play this game, the chief reason being that I am such a rotten loser. In fact, my tantrums would make John McEnroe seem like Mary Poppins in comparison. Mind you, I do hold an admiration for anyone who does excel at this energetic game. We are very fortunate to have a number of excellent tennis clubs in our area, those at Lee-on-the-Solent and at Alverstoke in particular providing good facilities. The Alverstoke Lawn Tennis Club has been in existence for over one hundred years, expanding to it's present position of being able to provide six grass courts, three outdoor hard courts and an indoor court. Squash and badminton courts have also been added over the past ten years. The club holds tournaments for senior and junior members every June, and a grand open tournament at the end of July, the latter attracting players from all over the world. Of course, those who only feel the urge to play tennis occasionally can use the public courts at Stokes Bay, kindly provided by the Gosport Borough Council in the 1920's. These courts were the scene of quite a commotion in 1932, this was when the council decided to open the tennis courts and putting green at Stokes Bay on Sundays. Although they were not opened until one o'clock in the afternoon, many religious bodies protested strongly that they should not open at all on Sundays, stating that it was sinful to do such things on the Lord's Day. Although it was all rather nasty at the time, the protestors had recently more or less lost their battle against picture houses opening on Sundays, so they were not liable to succeed with tennis.

Whilst we are in the vicinity of Stokes Bay, it would be a good opportunity to take a look at the famous golf course there. This club has been in existence for nearly one hundred years, founded in 1885 it was one of a limited number of courses in the country at that time, and is only two years younger than the club on neighbouring Hayling Island. It began as a United Services Club with nine holes, but later became an 18-hole course when it was linked with Alverstoke Ladies Club, who had their own nine-hole course laying west of the Long Water area at

"Jolly Hockey Sticks" 1908.

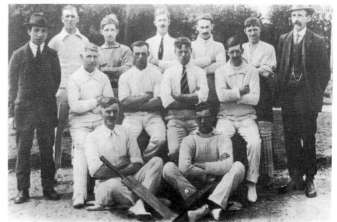

St. Faith's Cricket Team 1924c.

The Carnarvon Road Billiards Club.

Gilkicker. With the exception of a few honorary civilian members, the club was operated for services only for many years. When the Borough Council had the moats filled in, part of the course was flooded and had to be reduced to nine holes, but it is hoped that future plans will include extending the course.

It was during it's days as a services only course, that the famous Colonel Bogey legend emerged. A naval officer coined the expression 'bogey' for playing a hole or course in a reasonable number of strokes. When he was transferred to Haslar Naval Hospital, he used the expression whilst playing on the Stokes Bay course, only to be informed by a naval captain that as it was a service course, Bogey should have rank. Hence the Colonel Bogey legend. Within a few years the idea of Bogey competitions caught on, and was adopted by every golf course. And of course, need I remind readers of the renowned marching tune that evolved in the form of 'Colonel Bogey'.

The success of the Stokes Bay Golf Club in more recent times has been largely due to the efforts of the Club President, Rear-Admiral Ronald Paffard, C.B., C.B.E. It was truly a proud day for the Admiral when a new clubhouse was opened in 1979, replacing a structure that dated back to the early days of the club. We may now look forward to the club centenary celebrations in 1985, and wish them good fortune for another hundred years. As a final note, it is interesting to recall that the golf course at Stokes Bay drew complaints in connection with Sunday playing, this happening as early as 1907. However, the protest was not on religious grounds, it was made because several local residents thought that it interfered with other peoples enjoyment! By the way, the miniature golf course, or putting green, opened at the Bay in 1925, but I hardly imagine anyone will want to celebrate it's Diamond Jubilee!

The final sport in this section does not concern the striking of one ball, it comprises several balls. Ah, now I bet that has got you puzzled! Readers with flour-white complexions and bags under the eyeballs will know immediately that I am referring to the indoor games of snooker and billards. To say that Gosport has experienced a snooker boom in recent years must be an understatement, for no less that five clubs have opened in the town in a period of three years. The rise in popularity of this sport must, once again, be attributed to the employment situation. It also accounts for the fact that it is given so much afternoon viewing time on television. If anyone has any doubts about my theory, I will remind them that the last great billiards and snooker boom was back in the depression years of the 20's and 30's. So much for the bad news, the good news is that just as the previous boom produced players such as Joe and Fred Davis, the latest trend will undoubtedly bring new talent to the fore. The rapid rise of Steve Davis will I am sure inspire many others.

Apart from Steve Davis's cherublike features, players appear to be getting younger and younger, in fact, I harbour a notion that they will soon have to stand on beer crates in order to see over the edge of the table. This trend to youth is not really new, for George Collins began playing billiards when he was only six years-old. Who is George Collins? I hear you cry. Okay, all will be explained, stand by for the George Collins story. Born in 1845, through his dedication to the game George became famous in Gosport and Portsmouth sporting circles. In later years he developed into a national figure, and twice won the title of All-England Billiards Champion, his great years being 1877 and 1888. He once played billiards with Tom Sayers the great boxing champion. I would have been inclined to let the giant Sayers win the game, but George went in 'Where Angels Fear To Tread' and smashed him all over the table. A brave man indeed was our George.

George Collins returned to this area in 1899 to take-over as manager of the 'Arst Club' in Portsmouth. Whichever way you look at it, this was rather an unfortunate name for a club in a naval town! However, whilst working at this club George found time to play exhibition matches around the South Coast, he specialized in playing one-handed as a gimmick. Don't ask me how he managed it, the mind boggles! He once played on the Royal Yacht 'Britannia' for royalty, and it was during this exhibition that something really amazing happened. He was just about to play a tricky shot when the ship rolled badly, resulting in every ball on the table disappearing down a pocket. One of the funniest incidents in his long career occurred when he was enjoying a night off in the Sergeants Mess at the Victoria Barracks. A professional billiards player had been hired to give an exhibition in the Mess, but when he arrived it was revealed that there was not a player in the regiment good enough to take him on. The pro did not realize this, so the cunning sergeants bundled George Collins into a backroom and dressed him in a Trumpet-Majors uniform. Back in the billiard room, he was introduced to the pro, who had no idea who George really was. With a show of generosity, the pro loudly proclaimed that he always conceded 250 points in 750 to soldier players. George humbly accepted, and replied with a break of 137! He naturally went on to easily win the match, much to the amazement of the pro! Yes, George Collins was a marvellous character, and it was a sad day when he died in his Gosport High Street home in 1929.

As mentioned earlier, snooker and billiards clubs prospered in the 1920's and 30's, and Gosport had a fair number of them battling in the local leagues in those days. Many of them were associated with political clubs, or working mens clubs, but there was the odd club that was formed by friends or neighbours for the sheer fun of it. The Carnarvon Road Billiards Club was one such club, formed before the war, they originally played in an old bakery previously owned by the Allen family. Before it could be used for billiards, the chaps had to move out the old bakery oven to make space for the table. At least they had some expert advice available, for baker Harry Allen was also a member of the club. Other club stalwarts included Jack Land, and my old transport friend Cyril Fletcher, but I would imagine that there are still a number of old members residing in Gosport who have fond memories of the Carnarvon Club.

Jim Fuge.
Champion bowler and boxer.

THROWING THE BALL AROUND

fter all the running around in the first two sections, I feel that we should take things a little easier by looking at a less energetic sport. What better than the gentle game of bowls? Personally, I look forward to the years ahead when I hope to be in a position to devote some time to this relaxing pastime. Most of us at some time or another get the feeling of wanting to get away from it all, even if it is for only an hour or so. Living in a town or city, it is even more difficult to find a haven away from the hustle and bustle of life's busy throng. Perhaps this is why the game of bowls is so popular, for, even in a traffic-torn city it is possible to find one of these havens where, once inside the fence, one can sit and listen to the tap of wood against wood, set on a base of lush green turf, with the occasional murmur of appreciation from the players as they pace from one end of the rink to the other. A more peaceful and tranquil scene would be hard to find. Oooooops! Sorry readers, I almost fell asleep at the typewriter!

Although it does not usually take place on grass, or outdoors, I suppose that the nearest game to bowls is skittles. Back in the last century, this game was very popular in Gosport, and many of the public houses and taverns in the town had skittle alleys at the rear of the premises. Mind you, they had to have large backyards, some of these structures could be up to 60 ft long. Although the number of skittle alleys has dwindled along with pubs, I am pleased to say that there are still a few to be found around the area.

With the special turf and conditions required, the laying of a bowling rink can be a pretty expensive business, a factor that probably explains why we have not had many new greens opened since the war. Having said that, 1984 should see the opening of the long awaited bowling facilities at Lee-on-the-Solent. Bowling enthusiasts at Lee have had to fight long and hard for this green, so I am extremely pleased that it has at last materialized.

Although the opening of a new green is a rare occasion, the closing of an existing green is equally rare, and there are still a reasonable number of bowling greens hidden away in the area. Whether we have enough to cope with the demand that may arise through the increase in leisure hours in the future, only time will tell.

I would like to remind readers about a bowling venue that is sadly no longer in existence, yet in it's heyday it was the most popular meeting place in Gosport for the town's most prominent people. Not far away from the bustle of Stoke Road, and but a few short steps down Queens Road, that is where one would have found the Queens Bowling Club in years gone by. It was more than a bowling club, it was an institution where local folk, especially trades people, could meet and have a friendly chin-wag over a game of bowls or whilst partaking of refreshment in the pavilion. Just as golf may be used for the same purpose now, it is a fact that many business deals were clinched in the unique atmosphere of the Q.B.C.

The club was not always sited in Queens Road, prior to 1914 they had to make do on a spare piece of ground in nearby Sydney Road. But, even in those days it was a thriving club, and could boast a very formidable team of bowlers. They travelled around the country playing in various leagues and competitions, each away match being conducted more on the lines of a social outing. The year of 1907 was one of the most successful for the club in the Sydney Road period, not only because of the magnificent summer weather and their most pleasant trips across to the Isle of Wight to play, but also because they managed to pick up a few trophies and cups.

It was a particularly proud day for the club when their new ground in Queens Road was opened in 1914. As he had been chairman of the club since 1911, it was natural that Jesse Lee should be called upon to officiate at the opening. He emphasized how fortunate they were to have such commodious accommodation, and paid tribute to the excellence of the green and to the good work of Mr. Nicholson who had laid it so painstakingly. The setting was enhanced by the artistic pavilion, built by club member Mr. Osgood. But of course, none of this would have been of any use without the ground to erect it on, and the club was indeed fortunate that it had been provided through the generosity of William Hobbs, who was associated with the well-known firm of wine and spirit merchants. Anyway, following the opening speeches on that auspicious day of May 22nd, 1914, the first bowl on the new green was sent down by George Dukes, who was at that time Chairman of the District Council. As it was a Wednesday afternoon and half-day closing for shops, you can be sure that there were plenty of spectators gathered to cheer George on. There followed a session of bowling from five ends, following which the dignitaries adjourned to the pavilion for a splendid tea. The celebrations did not cease at this point, for everyone was invited to stroll along to the Olympia Theatre on the corner for a grand concert. This included much local talent, the top-of-the-bill spot being filled by the Widor Quartette, described as four ladies performing refined music with vocal refrain. To me, this immediately conjures up a scene of prim ladies in various shapes hacking away on violins and cellos, set against a background of potted palms and aspidistras! Still, it was much appreciated by the large audience, and finished off what had been a perfect day.

But, there were many more happy days to follow at the Queens, and nights as well, for the clubhouse was well employed on winter evenings for social functions and games such as billiards and whist. The devious male members of the Q.B.C. kept on the right side of their good ladies by holding 'Ladies Days' every season, in which the girls not only showed what they could do with the bowls, but were also entertained and given a mouth-watering strawberry tea. As Louis Lawrence, the well-known photographer in Gosport was a prominent member of the club, you can be sure that there was no shortage of pictures taken at such events.

Under team captain Jim Smith, our old friend from the 'Royal Arms', the bowling section went from strength to strength. But, it had to end, the war came along and the bowling green gradually deteriorated. Unfortunately, although it continued as a social club, bowling ceased after the war, and the green was replaced by a car park.

Just before he passed on to that 'Great Classroom in the Sky', I recall my old schoolmaster friend Frank Small telling me about the many wonderful hours he had spent bowling at the Anglesey Gardens Club. Frank was a past president of the club, and I know that he was awfully proud of the splendid plate that members presented to him on the occasion of his 90th birthday. The Anglesey bowling club has been in existence for many years, and during that time it has enjoyed a fair measure of success. Mind you, things were not quite so happy back in 1927, the lady members of the club turned rather nasty. The problem was that they thought that they were being fobbed-off with the poorer rinks at Anglesey, never being allowed to play on the better ones. The matter was eventually resolved, but not until many heated verbal exchanges had taken place.

On the other hand, the Alverstoke Club on the other side of the creek in Gosport Park knew how to keep in the good books of their lady members. They let them win! It's true, at a special match in 1928 the ladies beat the men at bowls quite handsomely. Just to show that they did not hold a grudge, the sporting

Queens Bowling Club.

Ladies Day Q.B.C. strawberry tea.

Prominent members of the Q.B.C.

Opening of new golf clubhouse at Stokes Bay 1979.
Photo J.C. Lawrence & Sons.

Opening day, Forton Rink, 1980.
Photo Fred Hughes.

gents entertained the gals to a magnificent strawberry tea afterwards at the Park Hotel opposite. Cor, I think that is taking sportsmanship too far! By the way, this club is officially known as the Alverstoke Old English Bowling Club. What is the difference between Old English and normal bowling? You may ask. Well, evidently they have funny shaped balls. Now now readers, stop that sniggering, I meant that they use differently shaped bowls, thus enabling them to get more curve on delivery. Also, there is no ditch or touchers in the Old English game. Now, that would not suit me, I like plenty of touchers in any game. In the later section on boxing, I have mentioned Jim Fuge's fine record with the club, but another name that is worthy of mention is that of Ted Jones, who was the hard-working club secretary for sixteen years until his retirement from the position in 1982. I will never forget the hospitality shown to me by club president Len Crouch, the oldest serving member, Cleveland Duffett, and indeed all club members when they invited me to a special presentation. On this occasion, Jim Fuge's daughter Mabel presented the club with a commemorative seat in memory of her father. Mabel was given the honour of bowling the first wood, and to everyone's amazement the bowl grazed the jack by the width of a finger nail! As Mabel commented, it was almost as if Jim had given a guiding hand!

To bring the record right up to date, Gosport borough at present has five bowling clubs, the Alverstoke Bowling Club at Gosport Park, the Gosport Bowling Club in Anglesey Gardens, the Bridgemary Bowling Club at Cunningham Drive, the Rowner Bowling Club on Rowner Green, and the Forton Bowling Club at Forton. As mentioned earlier, this number will be increased to six when the first wood is bowled at Lee.

The mention of funny shaped balls a little earlier on, reminds me of that rough and tough pursuit we know as rugby. I was not really sure which section to put this sport in, for the ball is both kicked and thrown. Or is it the players that are kicked and thrown? Either way, here it is. Contrary to popular belief, rugby is not purely swigging beer, singing bawdy songs, or generally raising hell, there is actually a game involved along the way. If there is a sport that rates the title of 'A Real Man's Sport', then it has to be rugby, and having the desire to keep my nose reasonably straight and my bones unbroken, I would not play this game for all the tea in China! Therefore, cowards such as myself may rejoice in the fact that the town has a fine rugby team in Gosport & Fareham Rugby Football Club. This club has been in existence for many years, and they can be seen battling away on their home pitch at Gosport Park during the season. Because of the many service establishments in and around Gosport, rugby is a particularly competitive game in this area, so any club that excels in this sport has to do it the hard way. As I said, it is all a bit too rough for me. Having said that, there is one aspect of the game that I would excel in. That's right, swigging beer, singing bawdy songs, and generally raising hell!

ENTRY OF THE GLADIATORS

The year is 1814, a brilliant August sun illuminates a curious scene on the green turf adjoining the beach at Stokes Bay. A large crowd is assembled, money may be seen passing hands, and the general atmosphere is full of excitement and great expectation.

Suddenly, a loud cheer rose from the gathering, greeting the six-foot frame of Tom Bessant. Tom was a well known Gosport waterman, so he had plenty of friends and supporters in attendance that day. But, hardly had the applause died when another cheer went up, even louder than before. The giant form of Henry Batchelor entered the ring that had been formed by a human chain. A member of the Gosport Press Gang, Henry was undoubtedly the favourite to win the ensuing brawl. His popularity was certainly not attributed to his sparkling personality, it was because of his massive physique.

Batchelor scowled across the arena at his young opponent, then to roars of encouragement from the crowd the two men closed, the battle was on. Even above the babble of the spectators, the sound of bare knuckles striking flesh and bone could be heard. It soon became apparent that the experienced Batchelor was an ugly customer to come up against, for he tried every dirty trick in the book. Round followed round, each terminated by a knockdown or a throw over the knees. Young Tom Bessant went down time after time, but bravely dragged his body back for the next round. Batchelor knew that he had the advantage, and strutted around the ring making sneering remarks about his opponent.

Tom held on, and by the 25th round it became evident that he was far from finished, and was in fact giving the bigger man some of his own medicine. Batchelor was smashed to the ground in the 25th, the 26th, and the 27th rounds. His face was covered in blood, his legs were not capable of supporting his bulk, and Batchelor had lost his stomach for fighting. To jeering from his supporters, he indicated that he did not wish to continue. Young Tom was hoisted onto the shoulders of his friends, and even managed to produce a smile from his blood spattered features as he was awarded the ten guineas prize money. That was some fight, but what a way to earn a crust! Being the natural coward that I am, I would say that he was welcome to it!

Although I have a strong aversion to having my own nose squashed, I have no objection to other people trying to distort another's features, in fact I have a great admiration for dear old Henry Cooper, a true gentleman of the ring. Of course, since retirement Henry has learnt a few more words, such as "You Splash It All Over' whilst waving a can of deodorant. But I preferred him back in his fighting days when his vocabulary only stretched to: "Well, eee's a good strong boy, but I'll git 'im in the next round"! Ah, the boxing memories come flooding back, all the family gathered around a battered old wireless set, the loudspeaker emitting such revered names as Tommy Farr, Joe Louis, Eric Boon, Freddie Mills, Bruce Woodcock, and Jersey Joe Walcott. One fight that I shall never forget was when Nel Tarleton defended his title against Al Phillips, more popularly known as the 'Aldgate Tiger'. What a scrap that was, by the 13th round young Al was a shade ahead of the veteran champion, but in the 14th he developed leg cramp and could only stand in the middle of the ring whilst Tarleton picked him off until the final bell, and subsequently retained the title.

I do not suppose that there are many people who realize that the legendary Joe Beckett came from this area, he was actually

Fred Mills.

Famous boxing brothers.

Pat Mills.

born in Wickham in 1894. Many of the old fighters had to learn their craft the hard way, usually through fairground boxing booths. As the Beckett family were fairground workers, Joe also developed his skills from the tough background of booth fighting. The rest is sporting history, he went on to become British Heavyweight champion, his fights against Bombardier Billy Wells and French Champion George Carpentier being particularly memorable. I am pleased to say that Joe was one of the few boxers to look after his money, and lived a contented life until his death in the 1960's.

I also count myself fortunate to have met a man who actually stepped into the ring to swop punches with Joe Beckett, the late Jim Fuge. Jim enjoyed an outstanding sporting life, and could be included in almost every section of this book. He was a very useful boxer, and built a good reputation in his younger days in local halls in Gosport and Portsmouth, holding his own against some of the best. His bout with Joe Beckett arose when Jim paid a visit to Wickham Fair around 1911, Joe and his brother George ran a boxing booth in those days, so when they asked for volunteers, Jim jumped at the chance. Although he was some four years older than the up-and-coming Beckett, he managed to give a good account of himself, and could take pride in completing the bout against such a strong opponent. Jim Fuge was a former member of the Gosport Harriers, and was also prominent in local football and hockey teams. With the outbreak of war in 1914, he joined the Gosport Battalion of the Royal Field Artillery, known locally as the 'Gun-Runners'. The Battalion went to India, where Jim continued his sporting interest by becoming a physical training instructor at the Gymnastic School of India. On returning to Gosport after the war, he resumed employment at Priddy's Hard, where he stayed for 43 years. During his service there, he was one of the crack-shots in the depot's rifle team. In retirement he played bowls at the Alverstoke Bowling Club, and was still playing shortly before his death in 1979 at the age of 89. It was quite remarkable that in his last season he won no less than four cups.

Whilst still on the subject of old soldiers, I ought to mention two well-known local chaps who were stationed at Fort Brockhurst, Jim and Albert Pike. They were both great little boxers, and earnt quite a reputation for their pugilistic efforts, in fairground boxing booths and around the local halls. It is a remarkable fact that Albert Pike was still fighting in the booths at the age of 63, and in the end they had to make him a referee in order to stop him putting the gloves on!

Boxing in Gosport was probably at its most popular stage in the 1920's and 30's, and the town could certainly boast a wealth of talent. I have already mentioned Wally Barnes in the section on football, both he and his brother John were excellent young fighters. And for good measure I will throw in the names of Roy Little, Tom Clarkson, and Taff Lewis. But there is one other name that will always be associated with the sport in Gosport, that name is Mills. Two outstanding boxers emerged from this family, Fred and Pat Mills. I usually refer to Fred as the 'Fighting Cobbler', for the family have been in the boot and shoe trade for many years, with John Mills still carrying on the business in Stoke Road. His father, Fred, was respected by every opponent who put on gloves against him, and I think that it would be true to say that he did more for boxing in Gosport than any other man, not only as a fighter, but also in promoting the sport and generally encouraging youngsters in it.

Fred Mills fought all over the South, and the bouts usually went his way. His love for the fight game did not dwindle as he got older, for he was still gracing the ring when he was in his late 30's. One of his most memorable encounters was against the renowned European Champion, Bugler Lake, it was supposed to be an exhibition match, but eventually turned out to be anything

Gosport Swimming Baths in pre-war days.
Lad in foreground displays his 'B of G' hired costume.

but. The week prior to the bout Fred was involved in a nasty car accident which left him badly bruised, but it is typical of the man that he not only climbed through the ropes to take on Lake, but also gave a good account of himself, landing some pretty nifty punches to the champion's jaw. Bugler Lake was none too happy about this state of affairs, and at one stage he turned to the referee, who happened to be Jimmy Wilde, former Fly-weight Champion of the World, and said: "Look ref, who is giving this ruddy exhibition, him or me?" Sadly, during the Second World War Fred got caught in a bombing raid on Gosport, and lost one of his legs. He still continued cheerfully with his cobbling, and I would expect that there are still quite a number of townsfolk who remember seeing Fred in the shop, for he only died in 1969, aged 77.

Fred had a younger brother named Pat, and with a little more luck he could quite easily have become one of Great Britain's outstanding light-weight champions. Pat Mills was born in Gosport in 1901, he developed into a pleasant lad with a liking for most sports. When World War I came along he joined the Royal Flying Corps as a boy entrant, reporting to Halton for his initial training. Although he was an easy-going sort of chap, he was a champion of the underdog, and many barrack-room bullies learnt only too late that he was the wrong man to pick a fight with, for he was more than a match for chaps much heavier than himself. Allowed to pursue sports, he developed into a first-class sprinter on the running track and a footballer of some note. His skills at the latter resulted in a trial with Fulham Football Club, but nothing could match his love of boxing, and he won the L.S.B.A. and the Allied Services Championship for his weight.

After leaving the R.A.F. he toured the world, boxing in China, Japan, and Australia. He was improving all the time, and in Australia only lost two fights out of fourteen, winning the Australian light-weight title. On his way to America, he stopped off at the Philippines to win the Championship of the East. His first fight in the States was an absolute cracker, taking place in 1923 against a tough Philadelphian named Joe Tiplity. The American knew a few tricks about 'cutting' his opponents up, and Pat's nose was bleeding profusely from the 8th round on. At one stage he took three terrific right-handers to the jaw in rapid succession, but astounded the crowd by wading back and forcing Tiplity onto the ropes. They loved his courage, and booed loudly at the final bell when the decision went narrowly against him. Pat learnt a lot about the American style of boxing in that fight, and he was a totally different fighter when he had a return match with Tiplity a short while after. This time the crowd booed Pat, not that he minded, for it was his arm that was raised as winner at the finish. So, if you can't beat them, join them!

Our Gosport lad had hundreds of fights in America, and became a great favourite with the press there, his impressive list of wins earning him titles such as 'Pat Sock-em Mills', or the 'Fighting Irishman'. Bearing in mind his Gosport background, the latter is rather difficult to explain, but boxing did have a strong element of showbiz about it in the States at that time. I suppose it still has. Anyway, Pat boxed on the east and west coasts and even made several appearances at Madison Square Garden, fighting several top-liners, including the great Benny Leonard. He also had the distinction of defeating Ray Mitchell, the big American hope.

Pat Mills settled in California for a while, entering the production side of the movie business. Eventually he moved across the ocean to Dublin, where he managed an office for Universal Pictures. He really was a flamboyant character, an old R.F.C. pal of his from Gosport, Bill Crockford, recalls meeting Pat about that time on Stokes Bay Beach. Although his features were very leathery from his long string of fights, Pat was standing by a super white sports car, with a lovely young film starlet on each arm!

However, life had it's ups and downs for Pat Mills, and with all the Hollywood razamataz behind him, he went back into the services. This time he joined the Royal Signals, which just happens to be my old regiment. He was posted to India, and whilst there he won the middleweight title by beating the formidable 'Gunboat Jack'. But he did not remain in the army long, and returned to England and boxing. One of his first fights was in Gosport, this was in a special tournament at the New Barracks arranged by his brother Fred. Pat fought Tommy Phillips the Welsh Light-weight Champion, and he really was in cracking form that night, forcing the Welshman to retire in the 8th round. He also had a memorable battle with the renowned Jack Hood, but age was beginning to catch him up. But, he still had plenty of fight left in him, and in 1929 a new boxing sensation suddenly hit the northern circuit, his name was Pat O'Brien and he was knocking out all the young hopefuls in sight. Yes, it was our old friend Pat Mills. Those were bread and butter days, and you could get more fights under different names, unlike the modern boxer who has two or three fights a year. The old boxers never had time for training, they were too busy fighting! Pat was based in Darlington, this will provide some idea of his schedule: Monday – Pat O'Brien knocked out George Wills in 3 rounds at Newcastle. Wednesday – Pat O'Brien knocked out Farmer Jackson in 7 rounds at Middlesbrough. Friday – Pat O'Brien beat Jack 'Kid' Casey over 15 at Leeds. And so on!

Some day, the winning has to end, it is like the old gunfighter in the West waiting for the new Kid to come and take his crown. Pat Mills eventually settled in Oxford to become coach to the University boxing Squad, producing many fine teams. He was also a top referee for the British Boxing Board of Control. I must emphasize that Pat was not a punchy slap-happy ex-fighter, he was a thinking man who could be as cutting with the pen as he was with his fist, and had several articles printed in national magazines. He was at his best when writing in the local press, usually championing the cause of the underdog. One of his campaigns concerned a busy road junction in Oxford, he warned that a small child would be killed there if something was not done. Shortly following this somebody was killed at the junction, ironically it was Pat himself! He was knocked down by a car whilst riding his bicycle. This was very sad, for a doctor stated that his body was in superb physical condition for a man of his age, but you can't fight a car. That incident happened in 1969, the same year of death as his brother, Fred, so Gosport lost two of it's most outstanding boxers, and I very much doubt if we shall see their like again.

Before we complete our look at the manly arts, I feel that it would be apt to include a few lines on weight-lifting and body-building. Both these activities went hand in hand with boxing in the early days of this century, for the Gosport Physical Culture Club used to hold their meetings in the old Market House at the ferry end of the High Street. The club had their most successful year in 1905, when they staged a large show involving boxing, wrestling, weight-lifting, and displays of physical excellence.

I must confess to having dabbled at weight-lifting in my time, and even had aspirations of gaining the coveted title of 'The Worlds Most Perfectly Ruptured Man', but it was not to be. But seriously, Gosport has produced a goodly number of strongmen over the years, and enthusiasts such as John Copeland and David Wilson have won their share of titles on the physique scene. The sport has been kept alive in the area chiefly through the efforts of two men, Don Styler and Joe Feltham. The Don Styler Gym in Frater Lane has been resounding to the noise of pumping iron for over twenty years, and during that time Don has served the town well by helping to keep it's youngsters healthy and off of

Ald. Ben Kent.
Gosport's sporting mayor.

the streets, a fact recognized by the Leisure Services Committee when they awarded him with the Sports Personality of the Year title. Don Styler also began the Mr. & Miss Solent City shows at the Thorngate Halls in 1978, and they have proved to be one of Gosport's biggest sporting attractions every year since, bringing some of the worlds greatest muscle names to the town. The name of Joe Feltham has been associated with weight-lifting for many years, for his knowledge of judging and coaching has made him one of the foremost authorities on the sport in the South of England. Joe is also one of that select band who have dedicated much of their free time to encouraging youngsters to keep their bodies fit and healthy, and that is an important factor in most sports.

In the 1980's there has been a fantastic keep-fit revival, and almost anybody who can touch their toes appears to have set themselves up as a physique expert. Through writing books and making exercise records, folk such as Jane Fonda probably keep-fit just by carrying their money to the bank. Mind you, this idea of exercising to the sound of music is quite good, and even I quite enjoyed listening to my joints creaking to the sound of Henry Hall's 'Teddy Bears Picnic'. Unfortunately, some wag switched the record for 'The Overture to William Tell', and my body has never been the same since! Never mind, perhaps I am now eligible for 'The Worlds Most Perfectly Ruptured Man'.

SPLASHING AROUND

With Gosport's close proximity to the sea, it is understandable why many residents get their sporting pleasure through aquatic pursuits such as swimming, fishing, and sailing. In fact, on more than one occasion I myself have been advised to "Go and paddle your own canoe", or something similar. As it happens, I like canoeing, and I was the proud owner of one of the old rubber skin and wood vessels long before the introduction of the sleek and modern fibre-glass models. My passion for this form of craft stems back to my younger days, and an old movie called 'Sanders of the River'. My favourite scene from the film features tribal chief Paul Robeson paddling a canoe down a steamy jungle river, whilst splashing along, he warbles with his dark brown voice a song with words that sound like: "I Yeek O-ho, Sandy. I Yeek O-ho Sandy". This had a lasting effect on me, and some thirty years later I could be found paddling off-shore at Stokes Bay, singing "I Yeek O-ho, Sandy" at the top of my voice. However, because of complaints from fishermen and music-lovers, I eventually had to dry-dock my canoe. Not long after this I bid a tearful farewell to my rubberized version of the Titanic, I flogged it to our milkman for eight quid, including a puncture repair outfit!

There are a number of toughies who swim in the open all year round, and I am not only thinking about those folk who hit the headlines by having a dip in the Serpentine every Christmas Day, for there are many hardened enthusiasts who swim in the sea in summer and winter alike. Our old friend Stan Cribb from the football section may be included in this select band. I once knew a man with one leg who would break the ice on a pond with a pickaxe so that he could have his daily plunge. Once in the water he would beckon his faithful old dog to follow him into the water, but the dog never did. It had more sense!

Ice has a great fascination for youngsters, and one of their favourite spots in the Gosport of yesteryear was the moat that ran by the Horsefield, now Walpole Park. One cold day in 1912 a group of lads were playing on the icy waters of the moat when suddenly, there was a loud cracking sound followed by a splash, a little boy disappeared from sight. His mates thought that this was the last they would see of their chum, but, to their amazement his head suddenly popped up out of another hole in the ice some distance from where he had fallen in. Apart from being cold and wet, he was able to toddle off home, where no doubt he got a jolly good hiding from Mum! Another young lad in 1929 was not so lucky, he fell through the ice in the model yacht pond and was close to drowning. Fortunately, his plight was seen by Newtown schoolboy George Hammerton, and without hesitation George jumped into the water to rescue the lad. Once the victim was safely out of the water, our shy 13 year-old hero crept away from the scene without any fuss.

Back in the 1800's, the town officials were very aware of the large number of residents who lost their lives through drowning. The figures were such that in 1875 the health authorities employed the services of a Mr. Tony to conduct regular classes in the art of swimming. Held at the Haslar end of the moat, the classes proved most popular, and of course, ladies were taught separately from the men. Lucky Mr. Tony! Mind you, when swimming then the ladies appeared to wear more clothes than they did when walking down the High Street. In 1900, a daring booklet on bathing was printed, this is an extract from it: "The chief drawback to swimming for ladies are the blue flannel costumes which, when saturated with water becomes awkward and heavy. The most commodious, and at the same time, most pleasant to the wearer, is a garment consisting of a dress and drawers in one. It should be made in grey serge, and have a band to confine the waist". Wow, I wonder what they would have thought of the modern bikini?

A hundred years ago, I remember it well, swimmers at Stokes Bay had a novel way of changing into their swimming gear. Prospective swimmers could hire one of the coastguard rowing boats, row out a short distance and drop anchor. Then, out of sight, they would change into their bathing togs, then jump into the sea and swim back to the beach, where they would rest and sunbathe. This was followed by a return swim to the boat in order to change back into their street clothes, then they would pull up anchor and row back to the shore. Now, this all sounds very nice, but just imagine what it was like changing in a small rocking boat with the flowing dresses and masses of petticoats that they wore in those days. I bet it made comical viewing, especially through a coastguard's telescope!

One advantage of swimming in Haslar Creek, could have been that you were able to obtain something nice for your tea, for in years gone by, oysters were stacked to some depth in the creek. Haslar Creek was also popular with the local lads for swimming, however, in 1919 this practice created quite a storm. Many complaints were made about the youngsters bathing nude in the creek, and several lady residents thought that it was quite disgusting that they should be subjected to such a degrading spectacle. Not much action was taken at that time, but a few years later the council solved the problem by building open air swimming baths not so very far away from the offending spot, on a site where the old town ramparts had once laid.

The Central Baths were opened on May 30th, 1924, and the good people of Gosport turned up in their hundreds to see this new addition to their rapidly expanding town. The baths catered for the needs of the 20's and 30's, providing a means of keeping clean as well as enjoyment, for many townsfolk then had still not got an adequate water supply at home. Nude bathing was not encouraged at the new baths, not for swimming anyhow, so anybody who was not fortunate enough to own their own costume could hire one. This was okay as long as you did not mind running around with 'B of G' emblazoned across your chest!

The Gosport swimming baths underwent a good deal of improvement work in 1936, the chief alteration being a new filtration and aeration plant, as well as additional buildings and changing facilities. Floodlights were also installed for evening bathing and regattas, this being quite a modern innovation for those days. Mayor George Ford was called upon to press the appropriate switches, and I am pleased to say that the floodlights and filtration plant worked okay. In the years immediately before and after the war, the baths were put to good use during carnival times, with swimming regattas and water pageants adding to the general merriment.

Gosport can be proud that over the years it has produced some jolly fine swimmers, and judging by recent competition results, I feel sure we have some potential champions now in our midst. In years gone by we also had some good swimming prospects, our old undertaking friend Eddie Crossland springing immediately to mind, for in his youth he swam for Hampshire. But, for sheer determination, one has to admire Sid Kent, who lived in Avery Lane. As a lad, Sid lost one of his legs in an accident, but it did not prevent him from swimming. He even played water polo, a very popular sport in those days. Sid died in 1938 aged 22, a short life maybe, but he crammed as much enjoyment into it as he could.

Model Yacht Club – opening day races.

Opening of Gosport Swimming Baths 1924.

Leisure Services Chairman Audrey Pearce awards the prizes at Gosport Angling Club. Photo J.C. Lawrence & Sons.

Making sail at Gosport Model Yacht Pond 1970's.

Since the war, many townsfolk have moved out of the main Gosport town area, with the result that a large portion of the population now live in the suburbs. Attendance figures at the Central Baths fell considerably, and it has been under threat of closure for more than a decade. Even as I write, the future of the open air baths is still under discussion. I am pleased to say that the Holbrook indoor pool that opened in the 1970's is still flourishing, and since opening, other facilities have been added to make it one of the best sports complexes in the Solent region.

I don't think that it would come as a surprise if I stated that the yachting world is linked very closely with Gosport, for the boatbuilding prowess of Camper & Nicholson is renowned throughout the world, especially during the inter-war years when they produced such great America's Cup challengers. But, Gosport is also famous for yachts of another class, model yachts. The lake in Walpole Park has for many years provided the venue for international model yacht racing, and attracts competitors from all over the world. On fine Sunday afternoons, it would be difficult to find a more pleasant scene than that provided in Walpole Park, with enthusiastic owners wearing jaunty yachting caps whilst plotting the fortunes of their treasured little vessels.

The Gosport Model Yacht Club has been in existence for over seventy years, their early meetings being held at the Nicholson Hall, this was just prior to the 1914–18 war. The meetings were presided over by Mr. Lapthorn, a much respected gentleman in the town, and the lectures that were given on model yachting by guest experts always drew large audiences. The club was about one year old when war broke out, so members had to wait another seven years to realize their ambition of having their very own yacht pond. Strangely enough, it was through the war that they eventually gained this facility, for with so many chaps returning home from the war with only the prospect of joining the dole queue, there was an abundance of surplus labour. Many men were kept gainfully employed on town improvements such as the Esplanade Gardens, the aforementioned Central Baths, and a model yacht lake. Sited on the old Horsefield, the latter kept them busy until 1921, and on completion it was reputed to be the largest artificial lake in the United Kingdom, comprising some four and a half acres.

The model yacht pond was officially opened in the August Bank Holiday of 1921, and over 3,000 people crowded into the area to join in the celebrations. Of course, there was a large gathering of local dignitaries to add pomp to the occasion, names such as Kent, Parham, Pook, Upson, Williams, Gillard, Windibank, Rogers, Masterman, and Lapthorn. Although he was chairman of the district council in 1921, Jesse Lee was unable to perform the opening ceremony, so Councillor Goodwin stepped into the breach. After he had duly proclaimed the pond well and truly open, followed by three loud cheers, the scene was set for the afternoon's entertainment. Naturally this included plenty of model yacht racing, with many visiting clubs taking part. Mr. W. Jackman was the racing events officer for the day, and Mr. Roak carried out the duty of official umpire. There were certainly some good prizes to be won, all donated by our local traders. Representing the G.M.Y.C. in the races there was Mr. Jackman's yacht 'Dorothy', Mr. Lock's 'Shelia', Mr. Baird's 'Doris', Mr. Mitchell's 'Betty', and Mr. Jurd's 'Scarlet Pimpernel'. You see, those chaps were not so stupid, they kept the little women at home happy by naming their boats after them. Mind you, I can't believe that Mr. Jurd was married to the Scarlet Pimpernel!

In addition to the races, the spectators were treated to a display by the Portsmouth Steamboat Club, and the fun was kept flowing by tub races and a water polo match. As dusk fell, there was a procession of illuminated craft, decorated with fairy lights and flags they provided a splendid finish to what had been a marvellous day in the history of the town.

Many more great days and events were to follow, with local spirits running particularly high in 1927 when the club won the coveted Yachting Cup, thus putting Gosport well and truly on the model yachting map. The win was largely attributed to Ron Jurd's yacht 'Gertrude', defeating the American yacht Bostonia II. But, probably the most satisfying event in the club's history took place in the 1920's when they challenged the professional skippers of the large J class yachts. The model yacht enthusiasts claimed that they could sail the big craft, but they doubted if the professionals could sail model yachts. The challenge was accepted, and I am pleased to say that the little people won the day.

The G.M.Y.C. may still have their greatest challenge to combat, in one of the town centre plans it was suggested that the pond should be filled in and replaced by a car park, or something similar. Only time will tell.

I guess that I had better move on to the big boys. I have previously mentioned Camper & Nicholson's association with the large racing yachts in those halcyon years of the 20's and 30's, and there is no doubt about it, it was a marvellous period in Gosport's sporting history. Although C & N built a great variety and number of craft, it was always the racing yachts that provided the glamour and hit the headlines. Vessels such as the Nyria and the Brynhild slid into the harbour from the Gosport boatyard to claim their share of fame, but it was the Shamrock's and Endeavour's that followed that really turned the eyes of the world upon Gosport. That spotlight was at its highest in 1914 when Sir Thomas Lipton's great yacht Shamrock IV was launched, with over one hundred gentlemen of the press arriving from London on a special train to record Lady Shaftesbury performing the official launch, followed by a slap-up lunch for 500 people in a nearby yacht shed. The ceremony was slightly marred for Tommy Lipton at the time owing to the fact that he was involved in an Old Bailey court case, the millionaire grocer being charged with bribery concerning food supplies for the armed forces. However, the war intervened, and subsequently saved Lipton's bacon. Sorry about that awful pun. The war also delayed Shamrock IV's challenge for the America's Cup until 1920, when she was beaten by the American yacht Resolute. But, Tommy Lipton was not the type to give up, and returned to the scene in 1930 with Shamrock V. Alas, this fine yacht also suffered defeat by the American's Enterprise.

Even so, just prior to his death in 1931 Tommy Lipton was making plans for Shamrock VI. It was left to Sir Thomas Sopwith to renew the challenge for the cup, and this he did in 1934 with the Endeavour, and in 1936 with Endeavour II. The latter probably came the closest to Britain winning the America's Cup. But, despite the succession of defeats, the races always generated great excitement in Gosport, with crowds of people lining the waterfront for launchings and race news.

Gosport is blessed with several flourishing sailing clubs, and the home waters of the Solent and Portsmouth Harbour provide an ideal setting for this popular sport. The Stokes Bay Sailing Club was formed just prior to the Second World War, and since then it has expanded it's facilities considerably to make it one of the best clubs in the South of England. Stokes Bay has also been adopted by enthusiasts of wind-surfing, which has probably developed into one of the most popular aquatic sports to hit the scene in recent years. However, these sail boards have attracted a fair amount of opposition, mostly from bathers near the shore, who look upon the boards as a potential hazard. Having taken a clout from one myself, I can only agree. This fairly new sport has also kept the Gosport & Fareham Inshore Rescue Service reasonably busy, for enthusiasts appear to sailboard all the year round.

Launching Shamrock IV 1914.

Back on the yacht racing scene, one of the keenest annual competitions that takes place locally is for the coveted Turk Trophy, with teams from the Lee-on-the-Solent, Stokes Bay, Royal Clarence Yard, and Hardway sailing clubs battling against each other. Although this series began in the mid-1960's, the actual silver gilt chalice trophy dates back to 1829, when it was made for the Portsmouth, Portsea, and Gosport Regatta. It was won in that first year by an officer of the Royal Navy, his yacht being named The Turk. The cup disappeared, but mysteriously turned up again 130 years later in a disused safe at Gosport Town Hall. Although the trophy only cost approximately £50 originally, it is now far too valuable for any club to keep for a year, so, after it has been presented to the winning club, it is taken back immediately and returned to the town hall safe until the following year.

This part of the coast is also famous for its sea fishing, and addicts of this sport may be seen adorning our beaches frequently throughout the year. The Stokes Bay headquarters of the Gosport & District Angling Club certainly attracts large numbers of fishermen to our beaches, and although there are many angling clubs in our region, I think that I would be correct in stating that along with the Elmore Club at Lee, the two are the largest clubs in the area. Founded in the early 1950's, the Gosport club at Stokes Bay can now boast a membership of over 400. The success of the club has been due to the enthusiasm of it's early members, people such as John Hunt, Fred Bartlett, Bob Lawrence, Ron Keetch, Angela Stafford, and Eddie Crossland. The club was also fortunate to have amongst it's members Jack Lunn and Arthur Daniels, for it was their building knowledge that resulted in the erection of a new clubhouse. Completed in 1979, the building was officially opened by that grand old man of the sea, Sir Alec Rose. Sir Alec happens to be the current President of the Gosport & District Angling Club, a position that was formerly held by Jack Lunn for seven years.

Back in 1921, there was a happening that was guaranteed to make any fisherman drop his rod and run for his life. 'JAWS AT STOKES BAY'. It is true, hundreds of people on the beach saw this deadly black body heading towards the shore, causing swimmers and paddlers to jump out of the sea with quite amazing speed. Well, wouldn't you? The deadly shark did not falter, it came straight on and left the water to land on the beach. When the many onlookers had gathered their nerve to move closer for inspection, it was found that the shark was not a shark, it was in fact a 21-inch type torpedo that had gone astray during a sea test in the Solent!

The time has arrived for us to discard our water wings, so I would be obliged if you would dry yourself off as quickly as possible, and follow me into the next section.

HORSE-PLAY

Just imagine what it was like in the Gosport of one hundred years ago, although the town area was congested, outside the ramparts it abounded in lush green fields and open countryside. Certainly there were the hamlets of Forton, Elson, Stoke, and Alverstoke Village, but the demon builder had not cast his net of bricks and mortar to any great extent. Outside the town, roads deteriorated into tracks, dusty in summer, muddy in winter. The horseless carriage had not made its noisy smoke belching entrance into the relatively serene and peaceful coastal resort that we know as Gosport. Yes, those were the days when faithful and seemingly tireless horses reigned supreme.

The horse fulfilled two roles, for it was an instrument of both work and pleasure. The work factor generally comprised pulling a varied selection of appliances, from carts and carriages to field ploughs. The pleasure aspect usually constitutes riding, and if anybody has any complaints about their particular lot in life, let them contemplate the fate of the horse, for they are probably the most sat-upon creatures on God's good earth. Mechanical contrivances have taken over the work load, so horses are now associated with leisure pursuits such as show jumping, racing, and dare I say it, fox hunting.

Although that square box that stands in the corner of most of our living rooms has almost succeeded in destroying many forms of pleasure and leisure such as the cinema and live theatre, in many ways it has had the reverse effect on sport, especially horse-racing. I can only assume that the average punter possesses a sadistic streak, and actually derives some pleasure from watching his money go down the drain. But not me, I must confess that I have always been a bad loser, I even cheat the kids at Snakes and Ladders.

In all the sport and leisure plans that have been proposed by the Gosport Borough Council in recent times, I suppose it is not all that surprising that a horse-racing track has not been included in the various schemes. And yet, would the idea of such a venture be so outrageous, for apart from Goodwood and Brighton, the South Coast does not exactly abound in race-tracks. Just imagine what a marvellous venue the airfield now occupied by H.M.S. Daedalus, and what a tourist attraction! Once again the idea is not impossible, for the Navy is not likely to be there forever, in fact the base was near to closing down in the 1970's. The great thing about sports such as horse-racing or golf, regardless of whether they are your particular cup of tea or within your income, is that they do succeed in maintaining open spaces, the green grass must be more acceptable than the concrete housing and industrial developments that have abused our landscapes in recent years.

The strange thing is, one hundred and fifty years ago, Gosport had a very nicely situated race course at Stokes Bay, rather similar to neighbouring Hayling Island. The course formed just one of the many attractions created by that amazing local entrepreneur, Robert Cruickshank, Gosport's answer to Billy Butlin. Robert had visions of his newly formed village of Angleseyville rivalling such illustrious watering spas as Brighton and Weymouth, and hoped to cash in on the new-found popularity of sea bathing by attracting wealthy patrons to this area so that they might dip their noble toes in the briny and stay around long enough to part with some of their not-so hard-earnt

Ready for the hunt.
Gosport & Fareham Beagles 1914.

money. This resulted in the erection of The Crescent with its imposing terrace of Georgian elegance, complete with adjacent gardens and a reading room. For those visitors with aquatic ambitions, a quantity of the very latest bathing machines were provided, and sailing regattas were held regularly.

As mentioned previously, a race course was added to the above attractions, the grand opening taking place in 1832. Over the following years, race meetings were held regularly during the season, and it may be assumed that many shirts were lost during that period. But, with Cruickshank's death in 1853, his various projects fell into a decline, the race course gradually became overgrown and the sound of punters cursing their rotten luck on the Gee-Gee's was never to be heard again.

Although it could hardly rate in the Top-Ten of sport, through patronage by persons of Royal blood, polo still retains a sizeable following. It is not a sport for the average sort of chap, and in days gone by it was only played by those of wealthy standing, mostly military gentlemen. As Gosport had a large number of military establishments scattered around the area, it was not unusual to see the sport being played locally. The main polo ground was sited near the Privett Roundabout, in the field opposite the petrol station, and many older residents have told me how they have seen several exciting games of polo played there in the days of their youth.

Another familiar sight in the pre-1939 years was that of horses and hounds chasing across the fields and farmland that surrounded the town, a scene that will never be enacted again because of the vast building development that has taken place in the last forty years. Many people would argue that hunting is not a sport, but I have no intention of getting into a debate regarding cruelty to animals. On the other hand, it was definitely regarded as a sport in days gone by, and as I am dealing with the past, I must include it in this publication. So, no bricks through my windows, please!

The most popular hunting group in our area was known as the Gosport & Fareham Beagles, and they flourished for some sixty years. Their story began in 1866, for it was in that year that a number of the local gentry got together over a glass of wine with a view to forming a hunting group. Mr Binstead of Peel Farm was elected as the first Master, but it was only to be for a few years, Samuel Blake taking over the position in 1870. The name of Blake is one that appears frequently in the local history of hunting, but many older readers will associate the name more readily with that of drinking, for the Blake's were renowned brewers in Gosport. Samuel Blake was Master of the Gosport & Fareham Beagles until 1881, and it was during his time that kennels were built near the Windmill Inn at Peel Common. It would appear that drinking and hunting were always closely linked, and many of the hunts began from local inns such as the Victoria Hotel in Lee, the Red Lion in Stubbington, or the Wiltshire Lamb at Bury Cross. Regarding the latter venue, it is very difficult now to imagine this busy area with huntsmen, horses, and a dog-pack waiting for the starting horn. With a cry of: "Horses stout, hounds healthy, earth well stopped, and foxes plenty", the hunters would drain their glasses and set the baying hounds free for the chase. Of course, although they liked to kid themselves that they were after foxes, the object of their chase was usually a poor little hare. If the hare had any sense, it would have headed for refuge in Anns Hill Cemetery, for the local authorities were not very keen on hounds running across this sacred spot.

The enjoyment of the day's sport very much depended on which route the quarry took, if it headed for Browndown the hunters knew that they were assured of good sport, for there were bags of open spaces. But it could prove dangerous for the dogs at times, for after the commencement of the Lee-on-the-

"Olympia Roller-Skating Rink", Stoke Road.

"Olympia Roller-Skating Rink", Hockey Team 1910–11.

Pulling together. Gosport Tug-o-War Team.

Solent Light Railway it was fairly common for dogs to run into the path of oncoming trains in their excited state. It could also prove tricky around Fort Gomer, for dogs would slither down the steep sides of the moat into the water, and subsequently drown if their plight was unseen. Our old farmer friend, Charlie House, did not always look kindly on the hunters and their pack, it was bad enough that they ran across his land, but he really took exception when his prize cabbage patch got trampled down, as it frequently was.

In keeping with the family tradition, Samuel Blake's son Frederick took over as Master of the Gosport & Fareham Beagles in 1889, and Fred can be linked locally with another sport in the form of golf, for he was captain of the Lee Golf Club for many years. Fred Blake remained a director when the family brewery was taken over by Brickwood's in 1926, he died in 1938 at the age of 71. His place as Master of the pack had already passed to his brother Herbert in 1912. But, the merry chase was to end, for after the war the demand for housing swallowed Rowner and Bridgemary, and the sound of "Tally-ho" was not heard again.

Although horses are no longer a common sight in the Gosport area, there are still a few private riding stables in existence, and I must admit that they add a little charm to the local scene as they canter across the grounds adjoining Stokes Bay. Mind you, not many folk are fortunate enough now to own their own horses, the cost of upkeep must be quite considerable. The ideal way to get a horse in the old days was through a local auction, many of the horses being released from duties with the various Government establishments or the Gosport Urban District Council. I have a catalogue of one such auction that took place in 1909 at the Great Coombe Meadow off of Melville Road, the proceedings being carried out under the direction of Messrs. Llewellyn, Puttock & Blake. There were plenty of horses on view, and in the subsequent auction the lowest price paid was for a Chestnut

Gosport & Fareham Beagles prize giving.

Cart Gelding named 'Bowler', who went for £6.6s.0d. The highest was for a Cart Mare named 'Blossom', led away for the sum of £44.2s.0d. By the way, for another seven pounds you could have had a dog cart to go with the horse, large enough to seat four, and complete with rubber tyres and cushions.

Although racing addicts have not been able to see their nags pipped to the post for over one hundred years in Gosport, at least they were able to go to the dogs at one time. Greyhound Racing in Gosport? Yes, it is true, the town did boast a stadium back in the 20's and 30's. The track was situated in the Forton district, at the rear of St. Luke's Road. Four meetings were held every week, with 14 flat and hurdle races for greyhounds and whippets at each meeting. I should think that it was quite humourous at times, occasionally any breed of dog was invited to participate for special races. The mind boggles at the prospect of terriers racing alongside poodles, and I am certain of one thing, I for one am not going to put any money on that dachshund, even if Prince Monolulu did say that it was a surefire cert!

*An adventurous outing to Lee-on-the-Solent for the very first Gosport Cycling Club 1887.
Just look at those bikes!*

ON YOUR BIKE!

feel sorry for the youngsters of today! Now, that may seem to be a strange statement in a world in which the great majority of kids seem to get everything that they ask for, from de-luxe bicycles to computers. But, regarding the former, they are very seldom able to gain maximum enjoyment from this marvellous invention, for it really can be frightening riding a bicycle on our modern traffic-infested roads, and country lanes are disappearing rapidly.

Ah, I will never forget my first bike. I will never forget it because I had to work so hard to get it! Up in the morning at six o'clock, and strapping onto my puny little body a bag heavier than myself in order to deliver newspapers through rain and snow. For my daily three-mile stroll I received half-a-crown a week, which I carefully stowed away in a cocoa tin, forcing myself not to flitter it away on the Dandy or Beano. Mind you, this did not bother me all that much, I read other peoples comics on the paper round. After what seemed like a hundred years, I was in a position to purchase the object of my affection, a gleaming Raleigh Roadster complete with dynamo lighting and Sturmey Archer three-speed gears. Every weekend, I would whizz off into an unsuspecting countryside on my two-wheeled wonder, and eighty miles later I would return home in time for supper. I usually ate the latter standing up, my rather sore little bottom making sitting down a trifle difficult!

The safety bicycle was probably one of the most revolutionary of all social changes, for it got people away from their homes, just as many years later television brought them back again. Cycling also gave women independence, and they were able to venture out without escorts. Dresses specially designed for female cyclists were adapted by Mrs Bloomer, and the cycles themselves underwent changes, cross-bars being omitted, and chain guards being added to stop long skirts from fouling the chain and spokes. Even so, these ladies were regarded as awfully daring, prompting one newspaper to report: "Two shameless females in bloomers bicycled through the village, and many of the local women were so shocked they threw stones at the riders".

At first, cycles had solid tyres, but later on inflated tyres were invented by a veterinary surgeon named Dunlop, and the bicycle became a more acceptable means of transport. This was good news for cycle manufacturers, and they had to work flat out in order to satisfy the demand for the machines. A couple of paragraphs ago I mentioned the name Raleigh, one of the most famous names in the history of the sport. This giant concern came about through the enterprise of a gent named Frank Bowden, a former lawyer. Frank became very ill, and doctors warned him that he did not have long to live. However, looking out of his bedroom window one day, he saw an elderly man cycling a tricycle around the square outside. Frank was amazed, for only a few weeks prior the man could not move his legs due to partial paralysis. Resolving that he had nothing to lose, Frank decided to get a bike and have a go, the result being that he made a full recovery in next to no time. He was so impressed, he decided to commence manufacturing these marvellous machines. He was particularly keen on the cycles produced from a small workshop in Raleigh Street, Nottingham, so in 1888 he became a partner and formed the Raleigh Cycle Company. By 1887 the old workshop had been turning out three cycles a week, but with Frank Bowden's influence expansion was rapid, and by 1900 the firm was producing 10,000 cycles a year in one of the largest factories in Europe. He was also responsible for the pioneering of the aforementioned Sturmey Archer gear system, allowing cyclists to ride up hills rather than walk up them.

So, by the turn of the century cycling was looked upon as a healthy form of exercise, as well as a pleasant and economic means of transportation. Cycling clubs sprang up in almost every town, especially in the South of England. The good people of Gosport were not slow at adopting cycling for work or pleasure, and could also boast of several clubs in earlier times, the largest of these meeting at the Vine in Stoke Road. There is hardly any need for me to add that Sam Tomlinson was also involved with this club, in fact there was hardly anything that he did not have an interest in. Gosport had one of the first cycle tracks in the country, and older readers may recall those halcyon days when the cycle track at Gosport Park attracted competitors from far and wide, including that great Olympic rider from Portsmouth, 'Clarrie' Kingsbury.

Gosport's largest cycling club originated in 1931, being formed by old boys of Newtown School. The key figure in the early days was Ern Reed, an enthusiastic cyclist who thought that a club comprising his old school chums had to be a good idea. It certainly was, although at this early stage nobody could have had the slightest notion as to how large the group would grow. They had no problems in providing a name for the new club, as Newtown Old Boys it was only natural that they should be called the NOBS. Headmaster Frank Gregory was also keen on the club being successful, and allowed the lads to use one of the Newtown classrooms as their headquarters.

The club started with eleven members, joining Ern Reed there was Harry Daniels, Bert Langridge, Harry Devine, Alec Cresdee, Len Lilywhite, Alec Titheridge, Bill Cline, Bill 'Polly' Parrott, and two brothers, George and Bill Carroll. Many of this group were shop workers, and as working hours were much

longer in those days, they had to wait patiently until Sunday came around in order to hit the road with their beloved machines. They would meet at the Wiltshire Lamb at Bury Cross, then off they would hurtle into the great big world outside the Gosport boundary line. Membership soon increased, and it became common to see happy hordes of cyclists heading out of Gosport in search of trees and fresh air. Perhaps I put that the wrong way round, for it was more vital to find trees on the way home, generally when one felt the call of nature. It was a marvellous feeling, not the call of nature, but of being able to escape from the confines of town-dwelling via the relatively motor-free roads of the pre-war days.

Ern was joined by his two brothers in the club, Jack and Walt Reed, and there were three other brothers, the Dougal boys, Ron, Dick, and Terry. Ron Dougal became well-known in the cycling world for his work as an official starter for the N.C.U. Charlie 'Flip' Willoughby is still associated with the sport as an official, he too was an early member of the NOBS. In his long career in cycling, Charlie served as secretary to the Gosport Cycling Club for over 30 years, as President of Fareham Wheelers C.C., and as Chairman of the Portsmouth Track League. He has been Chairman of the Wessex Division of the British Cycling Federation for over 20 years, this is the second largest division in the U.K. and promotes over 100 road and track races each year. Charlie Willoughby's list of service to the sport could seemingly go on and on, but I do know that he is particularly proud of the fact that he is the longest serving member of the Royan Sporting Committee, and is the only Englishman to be awarded the 'Medaille De La Reconnaissance Du Sport Cyclists" by the French Cycling Federation.

My old friend Vic Cox also has fond memories of the NOBS in his days of youth, and he still cherishes the many mementos that he won on his trusty old bicycle. Vic has numerous badges and

"Nobs" (Newtown Old Boys) Cycling Club 1931.

Erecting new clubhouse, St. Luke's Road.

Ern Reed in winning style 1954.

The lure of the open road. Gosport C.C. outing.

'Clarrie' Kingsbury.
Olympic Champion 1908.

Vic Cox enjoying a spin down
Gosport High Street, 1930.

awards for a variety of events, from hill climbs to track and road races. Inevitably, akin to most of us, Vic has swopped his bike for a noisy horseless carriage.

Eventually, the title NOBS was replaced by the NCC, Newtown Cycling Club. As the club expanded, headquarters were moved to a hall in Felix Road. Around this time, the club was open to lady members, something that Ern Reed was strongly against, but the vote went against him. As it turned out, it was through the club that he was to meet his future wife Nellie! Many couples met and married within the club, and later brought their children along to the outings to make it quite a family affair. The club toured all over the place, from the Isle of Wight to the West Country. One particular outing will be remembered by older members of the club, this being a four-day tour around the Swanage area. It rained absolutely cats and dogs the whole time.

Ern Reed still chuckles over one cycle outing around the Winchester area. The route included a very steep hill near Arlesford, with a nasty bend at the bottom, and several riders came-a-cropper and ended up in a ditch. Charlie Boult was one of these, his bike was wrecked and could only be regarded as a write-off. Whipping out a spanner, Charlie stood on a tree trunk and gathered a crowd around him. He then proceeded to auction parts from his cycle, following which he thumbed a lift to the nearest railway station in order to buy a ticket for the journey home with the money that he had raised.

After the war, under the banner of the Gosport Cycling Club, they went from strength to strength, the membership soaring to 160. They erected their own clubhouse in St. Lukes Road, this being an old prefab obtained from Portsmouth. Ern Reed was still cycling and racing, hitting the headlines in 1954 when he won a 25-mile road race at nearly 45 years of age. But, one of the club's proudest days was when three members, R. Dougal, D. Parfitt, and C. Harrison gained a place in the Best All-Rounders Team Championship of Great Britain, this being the first time that a local club had attained such an honour.

Sadly, touring by bicycle has been deposed by the family motor car, and like so many other clubs, the Gosport Cycling Club began to decline and eventually ceased. A few of the old members still meet for social gatherings, but there is no cycling involved, they can only reminisce about the good old days on the open road.

Before I close this section, whilst dealing with wheels I should mention roller-skating. What roller-skating? I hear you cry, but it is true, Gosport did have a very good skating rink seventy years ago. The Olympia Skating Rink opened around 1910, an event that was marked by a multitude of flags and bunting adorning Stoke Road. Although the rink was very popular for a few years, and even supported a fine hockey team, operations were eventually halted in favour of the new up-and-coming sensation, talking pictures. So, since then, roller-skaters have had to retire to the back-streets, or cross the harbour to the rink at Southsea. Of course, in more recent years we have seen the rise and fall of the skate-board, and the Gosport Borough Council in their wisdom had a skate-board park erected at Rowner, this proving to be a dead-duck with the rapid decline of the sport. Ah well, I suppose we can't accuse the Council of being cheap-skates!

I am pleased to say that there is a form of cycle sport that appears to be taking hold, and by recent reports one may conclude that it is here to stay. I refer to the new B.M.X. craze that youngsters have adopted so enthusiastically. The fight for a permanent course has been going on for some time, but thanks to the efforts of Doug Stanley, a course has been provided on ground off of Grove Road, let us hope that they can stay there. Anything that keeps youngsters from riding on pavements can only be good.

Having said that, as a kid I was probably one of the worst offenders. My chums and I also led park-keepers a merry chase by cycling where we should not have been cycling, and to me it always seemed that I was the one that got caught. I recall being brought to a standstill by a keeper leaping out from behind a tree and grabbing me by the collar. "Right, I'll have your name" he said. "Brown" I replied. "Come along lad, don't waste me time, give me your real name" he uttered. "Alright, you win" I confessed, and proceeded to give him the name and address of a rotten bully at school. To this day, I still wonder what the outcome of this incident was!

My final word on cycling is in the form of advice. Always lock your bike up well, and don't forget to have it stamped at the local police station. I remember only too well the plight of my poor old Dad, he saved up to buy a second-hand bicycle before the war. Wishing to do the sensible thing, he left the bike outside Woolworth's whilst he went inside to buy a padlock for it. That's right, when he came out the bike had been stolen! Anybody want to buy a cheap padlock?

The Finishing Line

We have now finished our sporting ramble, I sincerely hope that it has not tired you out too much. I do not profess to have covered every sport, or to have mentioned every club or individual involved in the sports that I have touched upon. At the same time, I hope that I have provided an interesting and entertaining reminder of some of the games and characters that abounded in the Gosport of yesteryear. Sport has an ever-changing face, with new clubs being formed, and fresh records being set every year. Of the more recent developments that have taken place on Gosport's sporting scene, I would say that the Gosport & Fareham Marathon is probably one of the most exciting. The man behind this popular road race around the district is Hugh Pritchard, who originally formed jogging sessions in Gosport Park. After running in the gigantic London Marathon, Hugh was inspired to organize the first local marathon in 1982. It was a tremendous success, attracting hundreds of runners from all over the country, and provided Gosport with a spectacle that it's streets had never witnessed before. Another marathon was held in 1983, and it is hoped that it will remain an annual event. Yet another new sporting development to take place in the borough, and probably the most unusual, is bicycle polo. A group of local enthusiasts play this exciting game on the Carisbrooke Field at Rowner, and it could quite well be the game of the future. In any case, cycle oil must be cheaper than horse oats.

Whilst compiling the sporting facts, figures, and pictures for this book, I was fortunate to have been afforded the help of a number of people. In this list I include Don Booth, Mr. & Mrs. B. Cooper, Colin Channon, Vic Cox, Stan Cribb, Ron Cross, Tim Farley, Dave Gasser, Ken Harrison, Jack Lunn, John Mills, Stan Mills, Ray Porter, and Ern Reed.

That is it, we have now reached the finishing line, and I sincerely hope that readers deem this book a winner.

"On the run". 1909 marathon down Forton Road.

Gosport Mayor Frances Behrendt proving that she cannot be snookered.
Photo J.C. Lawrence.